Eyewitness to Wehrmacht Atrocities on the Eastern Front

Eyewitness to Wehrmacht Atrocities on the Eastern Front

A German Soldier's Memoir of War and Captivity

Luis Raffeiner

Transcribed by Luise Ruatti
Edited and with a Foreword by Thomas Hanifle
English translation by Alan Donohue
Afterword by Hannes Heer

Pen & Sword
MILITARY

AN IMPRINT OF PEN & SWORD BOOKS LTD
YORKSHIRE – PHILADELPHIA

First published in Great Britain in 2021 by
PEN & SWORD MILITARY
an imprint of Pen & Sword Books Ltd
Yorkshire – Philadelphia

First published in German by Edition Raetia, Bozen/Bolzano in 2010

ISBN 978-1-39909-770-3

Typeset by Concept, Huddersfield, West Yorkshire, HD4 5JL.
Printed and bound in England by CPI Group (UK) Ltd, Croydon CR0 4YY.

Pen & Sword Books Ltd incorporates the Imprints of Aviation, Atlas, Family
History, Fiction, Maritime, Military, Discovery, Politics, History, Archaeology,
Select, Wharncliffe Local History, Wharncliffe True Crime, Military Classics,
Wharncliffe Transport, Leo Cooper, The Praetorian Press, Remember When,
White Owl, Seaforth Publishing and Frontline Books.

For a complete list of Pen & Sword titles please contact
PEN & SWORD BOOKS LTD
47 Church Street, Barnsley, South Yorkshire, S70 2AS, England
E-mail: enquiries@pen-and-sword.co.uk
Website: www.pen-and-sword.co.uk
or
PEN & SWORD BOOKS
1950 Lawrence Rd, Havertown, PA 19083, USA
E-mail: uspen-and-sword@casematepublishers.com
Website: www.penandswordbooks.com

Contents

Foreword:
Talking about the war

by Thomas Hanifle

A macabre spectacle: two Russian men and a woman dangle from the gallows in the main square of the Russian town of Maloarchangelsk. Men of the German Wehrmacht have hung a sign around their necks that reads in Russian: 'This is how partisans end up.' This is what happened in March 1942, with the camera held by Luis Raffeiner. Though photographing such scenes had been strictly prohibited by the Nazi regime, many of the German photographers in uniform nevertheless felt magically drawn to the atrocities in this war of extermination against Russia. The soldiers were unlikely to have been strictly supervised in any case. This is also suggested by recent photographic exhibitions in Germany, which hark back to such snapshots taken by former soldiers that until recently were gathering dust in attics or junk rooms.

In any case, Luis Raffeiner had no problems getting back home safely the film rolls and photos he exchanged with comrades or received from officers. Like treasure, he kept the photo material and other mementos of the 'Option'[1] and the war in a small box for decades. The photographs do not differ from what is commonly known from such albums. The predominant motif is the 'tourist's' view of the war: there are snapshots of comrades, landscapes, the Russian civilian population, or monuments in the occupied territories that make the war appear to be a safe excursion and were therefore explicitly approved by the Nazi regime. They were to be the link between the homeland and the front and thus strengthen morale decisively according to the calculations of Nazi propaganda. Pictures of crimes are largely missing from Raffeiner's collection. Also, that shot of those hanged in Maloarchangelsk, whom Raffeiner is certain he photographed: what happened? Luis Raffeiner had already had some film rolls developed during the war – he had usually commissioned comrades who were on home leave in Germany to do it. However, after the war he had entrusted around twelve rolls of film – Raffeiner reckons over 200 photographs – to his cousin, from whom he had also received the camera and the assignment to record impressions of the war. He got only part of the collection back, and then only after the death of the staunch Nazi. 'But these are only the harmless photos,' Raffeiner is convinced, and assumes that his cousin destroyed the remaining photos.

He could not remove the memories of what he had experienced, for these were burned indelibly into his mind. After returning home from the war, he told his family about them again and again, and every so often his acquaintances and friends too. At least, he told them those bits that he wanted to and could tell other people about. Even today, when recounting the stories, he takes refuge in saying 'You can't imagine it' when he has pictures before his eyes and cannot put them into words. Or he falls into the role of the observer who was not directly involved. From hints and insinuations, however, one can get an idea of how close Raffeiner must also have been to the brutal events, even if his memory sometimes lets him down after almost seventy years. By talking about the war, Luis Raffeiner tries to this day to come to terms with his traumatic experiences. In the immediate post-war period, however, hardly anyone wanted to hear about it – everyone was happy that the war was over. Raffeiner concentrated on his new life.

Decades later, two key experiences followed: in 1989 Raffeiner visited the 'Option' exhibition in Bozen/Bolzano,[2] which self-critically and for the first time officially challenged the South Tyrolean option of 1939 either to stay in the South Tyrol in Italy or to emigrate to the German Reich. Also discussed were the 'home-grown' South Tyrolean National Socialism and the inglorious role of many who opted to emigrate to Germany, such as the harassment of and agitation against those who wished to remain. Raffeiner did not find his story in the exhibition; his motives at the time for the option for Germany were not addressed enough for him. When he learned years later of the intention to turn the memoirs of the 'remainer' Franz Thaler into an opera, this was met with incomprehension. By fleeing to the mountains, Thaler had evaded deployment for Hitler's Germany, but was then arrested and finally deported to Dachau concentration camp. Right up to the 1980s the few South

Tyrolers who had said no to the Nazi state were considered by public opinion to be shirkers. Only after the publication of Thaler's memoirs in book form and the public discussion about them did the conscientious objectors receive a moral rehabilitation and, indeed, they became a symbol of the resistance. Raffeiner felt forgotten once more. Thaler's ordeal and, above all, the attention he received pushed Raffeiner's own fate even further into the background. He read Thaler's life story as a counterpart to his own: here a remainer, there a person opting to leave; here a deserter, there a combatant; here an anti-fascist, there a Nazi; here a hero – and what was he? He had been through a lot in the war and then especially in captivity. And he had never had anything to do with Hitler. According to Raffeiner, his own ordeal ought to have its place in history too.

During this time he set out his life story to Luise Ruatti, a young woman from Naturns/Naturno; they knew each other from their joint involvement in the local theatre association. Ruatti was impressed. Above all, she realized how little she and many of her generation knew about this part of (South Tyrolean) history. Thus, almost fifteen years ago she came up with the idea of recording Raffeiner's life for posterity. For two days they both holed up in the cramped, dark room of the local parish broadcaster 'Sankt-Zeno-Funk'. Raffeiner explained that Ruatti recorded his memoirs on tape and gradually put them down on paper, from which this book has now appeared in revised form. The result is an important document for contemporary history that deserves to be emulated, especially since the war generation is slowly dying out. In every village there are contemporary witnesses who still have a lot to tell – and in whose attics there is probably illustrative documentation that tells its very own story.

The Hamburg historian Hannes Heer, who caused a sensation in Germany in 1995 as director of the exhibition 'War of Extermination: Crimes of the Wehrmacht 1941–1944', was also won over for the present book project. Having read the manuscript, Heer agreed to make a historical classification of the memoirs – but not without first speaking to the protagonist himself. For two days he sat with the 93-year-old Raffeiner, reconstructed his unit's combat route with him, questioned discrepancies and confronted him with the horrors of this cruel war. His conclusion was that Raffeiner was no saint, as this war of extermination had made him both a victim and a perpetrator at the same time. 'But in spite of everything he remained decent and after the war he had the courage to bear witness to the crimes that he saw,' said Heer to one of Raffeiner's sons following the meeting. Luis Raffeiner has thus found his place in history.

Thomas Hanifle
Naturns/Naturno, June 2010

Chapter One

Monastery cell number 10

I was born in monastery cell number 10 in Karthaus/Certosa in the Schnalstal/Val Senales, a side valley of the Vinschgau/Val Venosta. It was in a monastery cell because the village had been built within the walls of the Carthusian monastery Allerengelberg. For four centuries, until the end of the eighteenth century, the devout Carthusian monks had lived here in twelve cell houses. That is why Karthaus is still commonly referred to today as 'Kloster' (monastery). My father's name was Josef Raffeiner and he was a son of the Oberleithof from Vernagt/Vernago near Unser Frau/Madonna di Senales in the far end of the Schnalstal. From a cousin he inherited the aforementioned 'friar's cell' in Karthaus and the small monastery mill by the stream below the village. Thus, he became the new 'monastery miller' and could count himself lucky, because whoever did not own anything had no choice but to become a day labourer. In addition, the Church would not allow somebody to marry if they could not support a family. So father took over the little house and mill and asked Aloisia Kofler from the Mühlhof in Katharinaberg/Monte Santa Caterina if she would be his wife. The wedding took place in Karthaus on 1 April 1912.

As a result, my mother brought a total of six children into the world: Josef in 1913, Anton the following year, and Maria in 1915. It was on 23 July 1917 when I first saw the light of day. In the summer of 1919, the year South Tyrol was officially annexed to Italy, our mother finally had the twins Luise and Peter. But none of our lights shone particularly brightly. I do not mean the fact that there was no electricity, only kerosene lamps, in our case the particularly economical 'Salzburg' lamps. 'Minimalism' reigned in every respect: with regard to food, clothing and especially money. It also did not help that my father did not have to go to fight in the First World War – he was the only miller in the village and therefore indispensable – as our little mill did not bring in much anyway.

Karthaus in the Schnalstal. Before the fire, the Raffeiner family lived in the house that was monastery cell number 10 (to the right of the church, the first house of the group of three in the picture).

There was barely enough to live on for the family of eight. People had their grain milled, and often the work was only rewarded with a 'thank you' as they had little themselves.

In Karthaus there was only one big farmer, called Sennhofer, who grew grain himself. His farm stands majestically above the village with a view far into the valley. People used to bypass his grain field with their cows, who would use the edge of the field to turn. This strip of land, the so-called 'Onawond', was leased to my father for mowing. In return, he had to mill Sennhofer's grain. People lived more or less through such barter. Because my parents did not even have enough land to support feeding a cow, they had to carry some of the hay home in racks on their backs. They even fetched the feed from the Vorderkaser, a farm in the neighbouring Pfossental valley. The entire effort to look after a few domestic animals was enormous.

My parents owned a cow, two goats, a few chickens, a pig and, in addition to the garden behind the house that had already served the monks, a very small uneven piece of land on the edge of the forest above the Sennhof. Our two goats grazed up there on the steep terrain. Our cows, on the other hand, were housed in a stable on the village square. The associated dung heap was certainly no ornament for the village square and probably bothered one or two people, but it was not the only one.

We used the manure as fertilizer for the meadow and garden: my mother mainly planted broad beans, cabbages and potatoes there. Since Karthaus lies above 1,300 metres, not much grew there. And vegetables like tomatoes were not even known yet back then. My mother got the cabbages from Platthüttl, a farm that lies between Karthaus and Neuratheis. At that time these vegetables grew much taller than they do today and only had a very small head. Each family had a barrel in which cabbage and beets were stored as sauerkraut for the winter. To the poor inventory of every household also belonged a *Stinkölbundel*, a kind of container which could be filled in the only shop in the village with kerosene for the lamp.

The village square in Karthaus. The Raffeiner family also had their stables and dung heaps there.

The bread was bought at the bakery, as only the farmers had their own oven. My mother used the grain – barley, oats and rye – to make soups and also 'mash', a nutritious porridge made from milk and flour. For the morning and evening meals there was either mash or a very thin *Brennsuppe* (flour soup): because it was so thin, we called it *Wosserschnoll* (water lumps). For lunch there was either potatoes, polenta, dumplings or barley soup. People usually ate from a pan that was placed in the middle of the table and from which everyone spooned out their food following a prayer.

The pig was slaughtered just before Christmas. The main part of it was smoked, and thus preserved in this way. Throughout the winter there was mostly cabbage and some meat, and only at Christmas even doughnuts filled with chestnuts and baked in pork fat. Unfortunately the portions were always too sparse for the whole family. By July or August the last bit of bacon was gone and we had to console ourselves with the thought of next Christmas.

My mother, like all other women at the time, did not have it easy: raising six children, tending to the garden, looking after the animals, and washing dirty clothes by hand. The few items of clothing that people owned at the time had to be constantly mended so that the younger siblings could reuse them. Only on Sundays was mending clothes not allowed. There was a saying for women and girls: 'Sunday stitches burn you!' By this was meant hell-fire. Sunday was very important, sacred, and the Church generally had a great influence on people's lives. After each birth my mother had to go to church for a blessing because women were considered impure following a birth. Even at the church door the priest began the elaborate ritual that helped the woman to regain her status of purity.

On Sundays the men met in the tavern after mass. There were two in the village: the *Rosenwirt* and the *Kreuzwirt*. My father was not much of an inn-goer and did not care much about politics either, which people liked to bluster about there. He often held back with his opinions, even when Italian fascism, with all its consequences, gradually established itself in the valley and in Karthaus too. He carried out the prescribed Sunday duties and on weekdays he worked in the mill. When a small power station was built next to our mill in 1923 to supply the village with electricity, my father took over care of it. He was happy about the additional income,

Luis Raffeiner with his childhood friend Bernhard Grüner (left). Grüner later became a staunch Nazi and functionary with the VKS, the *Völkischer Kampfring Südtirols* (a Nazi organization in South Tyrol).

Back of a photo. The friendship broke down during Raffeiner's leave from the front in July 1942, when Raffeiner expressed his opinion about the imminent defeat of Germany and thus aroused Grüner's hatred.

Nichts hat der Mensch so eigen

Nichts steht so wohl ihm an

Als daß er Treu erzeigen

und Freundschaft halten kann

Bernard Grüner

Pfossental, am 9. August 1936.

even if it was only small. His parenting technique was simple and efficient, like my mother's: 'If you don't obey, you don't get anything to eat!' That usually helped.

We children, of course, also had our duties. In addition to feeding the chickens we were responsible for the kindling. It was arduous work: we had to go up into the forest again and again, and the path was long and steep. The small amount of wood that we brought home was quickly used up again. From time to time we also took *Haislstreib* with us. These needles that had fallen from the forest trees were needed as litter for the outhouse.

We children mainly met on the village square to play. Tag and hide-and-seek, teasing, but then also scuffles were the order of the day. I preferred to hang around with Bernhard Grüner, and sometimes his sister Marianne also played with us. As a child I could not have known that this friendship with Bernhard would end tragically.

Chapter Two

A fire and its consequences

On 21 November 1924 a devastating catastrophe occurred in Karthaus. It was around 10.30pm and I was already in a deep slumber on my straw mattress when I was torn from my dreams with the words 'Up, up, it's on fire!' I did not understand at all what was going on. I stumbled out of bed, half asleep. My sister Maria helped me into my clothes. Hectic instructions were shouted back and forth, the most essential things were hastily gathered together upstairs and downstairs. I stood there being pushed aside because I was in the way. Suddenly Maria pressed something under my arm too, and I was chased out of the door with my other siblings. Outside I heard excited voices, the roaring of animals, steps on the stones of the monastery corridor, and dogs barking. Lantern lights flitted about, there was mass confusion. There was no time to look. By now I had understood what was going on. I was taken outside the monastery wall along with the other children. Father had assigned us a place below the village where the wall was highest. After he had retrieved the cow from the stable he hurried back to rescue the pig. When he got to the stable the roof beams had already caught fire, as he later told us. An Italian tax official tried to stop him from getting the pig, but my father pushed the man roughly aside and rescued our pig from the burning pen.

Meanwhile, I waited with my mother and siblings below the village. The high wall that protected us also blocked our view of what was happening. All you could see was the glow of the fire, which illuminated the night. The wind carried wisps of voices, crackling, and cracking down to us, sparks floated into the valley, and the smell of burning impregnated the air. Suddenly it shot into my head and would not give me any peace: I absolutely had to know if our house was also on fire. While Mother was busy with the younger siblings, I hurried along below the wall until I came to the place where there was a gap in the wall. From here I could see the flames that blazed from the houses. And yes, our house was on fire.

On 21 November 1924 the entire village burned down and the Raffeiner family lost everything.

I breathed a sigh of relief. 'Thank God, it was burning!' There was one thing that had been weighing on my young mind for a long time. For father owned a silver pocket watch, a beautiful heirloom, that he only wore on very special occasions. It must have been very valuable to him because he had forbidden us under the strictest threat of punishment to touch this watch. But I was an inquisitive rascal, and my curiosity was simply stronger than my reason. One fine day I gave the watch a thorough inspection with my pocketknife. With the tip of the small blade I un-screwed the tiny little screws. The cogwheels were so thin and delicate – I was fascinated by this technical marvel. So I disassembled the whole watch with the intention of putting it back together properly. Unfor-tunately my honest endeavours were not crowned with success. My ears burned when, after trying in vain, I put the dismantled corpus delicti back in my father's box. Since then I had been tormented by my conscience and even more so by the fear of punishment. So I was very relieved when I saw the flames because they obliterated the traces of my deed. That was my personal, childish perspective of this dramatic event. I was not aware of the actual implications of the flames. Not yet.

Back with my family, we spent the night there and then outdoors. It was the last hours of our being together. The fire had caused a devastating catastrophe that night: the whole village burned down except for a few houses, and the church also fell victim to the flames. Many animals could not be saved and perished wretchedly in the fiery hell. Two elderly people were killed in the fire, another died a few days later as a result of the fire. The cause of the fire has not been fully clarified to this day. Homeless and deprived of their few belongings, many families were close to despair. Many had relatives who offered shelter for the time being, but afterwards most families were torn apart.

In our case, the two youngest siblings, Luise and Peter, found pitiful shelter with our parents in the small mill below the village. In the mill there was only a small, secluded room, the *Mühlstübele* (little mill room). My mother slept with the twins in this neatly panelled room. The milk centrifuge just managed to fit in between the sleeping area and the wall. Father made a den for himself by the stairs that he could sleep in. Unfortunately we never returned to our house because our family lacked the funds to renovate it. After the fire my father refurbished the barn and my mother went up to the village three times a day for seventeen years to tend to the animals.

The rest of us children were given shelter by various farmers in the valley. Josef, the eldest, found a place in Gorf, while Anton stayed with the Spechtenhauser family on Oberörl. Maria was taken into my mother's parents' home at the Mühlnhof in Katharinaberg. The day after the disaster my mother also got me a place in the neighbouring village of Katharinaberg, at the Mittereggerhof. I was 7 years old and I still remember how she took me there and disappeared without saying goodbye soon afterwards. A bad time now began for me: the family did me no harm, but there was a farmhand living on the farm who made my life hell. Right at the beginning he made it clear to me that I had to 'follow' him – in other words, to obey him. I was utterly intimidated, and all too often my scrawny body felt his superiority.

I had to go to the stable with him every day and tend to the sheep. There he grabbed me and threw me like an animal from one sheep manger into the other. He had also noticed that I easily became dizzy. Now I had to go to mass with him on Sunday, and the way to church from Mitteregg to Katharinaberg led over a particularly narrow – and as far as I knew a very high – wobbly bridge. In the middle of the bridge he grabbed me and held me over the handrails. How I felt about this is difficult to describe. Fortunately I kept my eyes closed.

Every day was a nightmare: whenever he felt like it, he grabbed me, pushed me around, or hit me. And again and again I heard the threat: 'If you dare tell anyone about this you'll end up getting even worse treatment!'

How I would have loved to be able to confide my suffering to my sister. She was living with the farmer below the Mitteregger, at the Mühlnhof. When I saw her on the way to school, I would often start to cry. I even avoided her so that I would not be tempted to share my distress with her. That's how intimidated I was. Deep down in my young soul I felt abandoned by the whole world. The farmers were good to me, but they seemed to have no inkling about my lot. Only now and then did they wonder at my strange behaviour, especially when we were eating. My tormentor did not even grant me that. If he bumped against my foot under the table I had to stop eating immediately. He clearly enjoyed this game. No wonder that I was always hungry. That would almost have sealed my fate on a winter's day.

In winter, when there was snow on the road and it was difficult to travel on, we got to bring our school food with us – 'we' meaning the farmer's three children and me. There was a small piece of bacon and half of a hard *Paarlbrot* (pair bread). There was barely enough for all four of us, and mostly I got a raw deal. This time too I came away empty-handed. Then I remembered those children I had seen chewing pitch (resin) in the autumn at the edge of the forest. That seemed to me to be a brilliant thought. I ran up to the church. Above the Untermoarhof there was a 'Holzplum', a large pile of wood made up of larch trunks. I found plenty of bad luck there. I grabbed a small bit of this gooey mass and greedily began to chew on it. Unfortunately I did not know that only the natural resin from spruce trees was edible. After a very short time larch pitch was stuck all down my throat and I could not breathe any more. I writhed, cried and gesticulated in mortal fear. Fortunately for me the women from the Untermoarhof had noticed me. When I did not answer their call they immediately rushed to my aid. They cleaned my mouth and saved me from the danger of suffocation.

I felt the pity of these women: they suspected that I was not doing well. The sacristan, who lived with the miller, therefore invited me into the house every now and again. Mostly on Saturday, because that's when the baker brought her the bread. It smelled enticing as he went by, and the tips of the bread rolls looked out temptingly from on top of his basket. Then when the sacristan cut the rolls into slices for Sunday, a few bread-crumbs always fell off that I was allowed to eat. But not all at once, because she was afraid I might choke on them in my greed. Sometimes she would also give me a piece of bread.

The first winter away from home went by. My parents had never come to visit me. They probably thought it would be better for me that way. Except for one Sunday in spring. As always I had gone to mass with my tormentor. On the way home we came to a place that was once called the *Protzegg*. From here you could see across to Katharinaberg, and behind a bend you came through the valley to the Mittereggerhof. Here the farmhand felt safe as he once again played his cruel game with me. He led me around like a dog, beat me and slapped me. Then a resolute voice rang out from the forest: 'Now we've seen enough, we'll tell mother about this at home!' With that the farmhand immediately let go of me.

The next day, as it happens, my mother came and got me. She found me emaciated, neglected and deeply intimidated. There was no room in the makeshift mill, so my mother took me to another farmer that same day, to Obervernagt on the Raffeinhof. Warm-hearted people lived there, child-less themselves, who immediately took pity on me and began to nourish me with nutritious meals. But my body was not used to the lavish food and it rebelled. I was plagued by terrible diarrhoea and constant vomiting. The farm-folk even feared that I would die in the end. When my condition remained unchanged after a week, my benefactors decided in desperation to give me two more days. Otherwise they would carry me home to my mother in a basket. They only told me about this later, of course, because I actually began to recover and was visibly better. I was eating with a healthy appetite and enjoyed milk and butter. I spent this summer as well as the next three at the Raffeinhof – it was an unforgettable, wonderful time, for which I am still grateful today.

Chapter Three

Fascist harassment

I had been sent to school in Karthaus in the autumn of 1924, but soon afterwards the fire broke out. After that I attended primary school in Katharinaberg. When the second year of school began for me in the autumn of 1925 I was living with a family on the Oberniederhof in Unser Frau near the school. I could not stay at the Raffeinhof because the way to school from there was too far and too dangerous, which is why my parents sent me to live in Unser Frau. There was only one class, which contained all age groups. Now we children also came to experience the consequences of fascism. The lessons had still been held in German in my first year of school, but from now on this was strictly forbidden. The German-speaking teachers were all replaced by Italian ones.

When my parents' financial situation had improved somewhat, I returned to Karthaus. That was in 1926. Now the five of us lived in a very confined space in the small mill. We had neither a living room nor a kitchen, but I was just happy to be back with my family.

From that time on I attended school in Karthaus with my siblings. After the catastrophic fire this had been set up in a makeshift manner in Peter Grüner's house. There was space for around thirty children in one single room. Our teacher was a very young Italian, only 19 years old; I have forgotten her name. She did not understand or speak a word of German, and we did not understand a word of the lessons.

Many adults told us children that we should not put up with anything from the *Walschen* – which is what we always called the Italians.[3] My parents were unbiased and remained neutral in this regard. Nevertheless, this had no effect on us. The older boys annoyed the teacher, and we little ones felt encouraged by this. We supported them with roars of laughter because we earned their praise as their allies. Once it even went so far that a friend of my brother brought a pop gun to school and used it to shoot the chalk figures on the blackboard. We squealed with excitement. The

Primary school class with teacher Elsa Kohl and pastor Gottfried Alber. Luis Raffeiner is sitting on the far left in the front row. Karthaus, September 1924.

teacher became frightened and took cover behind the lid of the desk, which offered an even more tempting target. Now he took aim at this too. Then the room fell silent. You could hear faint whimpers. The teacher was crouching behind the lid of the desk, trembling and crying. The lads had gone too far.

Whether it was because of a guilty conscience, this girl's character, or some sort of warnings, I cannot say. In any case, the relationship was gradually loosening up. The lessons became more bearable for both parties, and were often even conducted in a creative way. The girls learned handicrafts and we boys were allowed to carve wood. For this we were also to bring a pocketknife to school in addition to the wood.

One day some men from the fascist militia who were stationed in Karthaus came to our school to check the pocketknives. The cutting edge could not be longer than the width of three fingers. Anything beyond that was forbidden. We students knew that, and so it was no real surprise that one knife or another got thrown straight out of the window. The fascists gathered up the carving tools and brought the parents to account.

Later, when I was older, a teacher from Riva on Lake Garda taught us and of him I have fond memories. Like all our other Italian teachers, he tried to make joining the Balilla, the fascist youth organization, attractive to us children. Admittedly, it was tempting, because who would not want to own a beautiful new shirt? But there was no point in asking my father, he had different worries entirely.

Apart from religious instruction, which took place outside the class-room in the cold church, we did not have any lessons in German. I never attended a so-called 'catacomb school' with illegal German lessons. After my schooling with Rosa Brugger, née Kofler, there was a catacomb teacher in Karthaus who taught the children a little German for a while. As she lived in the middle of the village, it was obvious after a while, even for the fascists, that she was regularly receiving visits from children. The teacher would have been punished immediately under normal circumstances, but Rosa was lucky. At that time Gualtiero Gentini was stationed with the fascist militia in Karthaus and he was in love with a girl from the village. It was thanks to this fact, but also to his humanity, that he emphatically warned the teacher and thus saved her from severe punishment.

One could still get used to the presence of the fascists in the village, but not to their reprisals. Most of the people remembered the later head of the fascist militia, Dalla Mariga, as unpleasant. The lives of the locals were spoiled by intrusions into the most banal aspects of their everyday life and sometimes made almost unbearable. Not only white stockings, the so-called *Stutzen*, but also the blue aprons were forbidden. A popular source of fun was the *Goaßlschnölln*, the loud and fast cracking of a whip. The fascists could not stand it at all, and so the whips were unceremoniously hacked into pieces.

I later got to know Dalla Mariga personally. I was already 20 at the time. One time the issue was about the dung heaps in the village square, which also included the one in front of our stable. Some villagers did not like these at all, and they complained about them to Dalla Mariga. He then summoned my father to the house on the village square that the fascists used as barracks. As he could not speak any Italian at all I had to go along with him. Dalla Mariga received us even beforehand from afar with a tirade of insults, and when my father reached the top of the stairs Mariga knocked his hat straight off his head with his hand.

Some time after this incident I had to go to the barracks once again. This time my father had ordered me to go there. He was in charge of the small power station in the village and probably knew that electricity was being used without permission – that is, stolen – for an electric furnace. The power station barely provided enough electricity for the entire village, so consumption was strictly and fairly regulated. Without exception. When I got there, I saw my father's suspicion confirmed. I therefore politely informed Dalla Mariga of the unauthorized use of electricity. He immediately grabbed my throat and shoved me against the wall in such a way that you could see his fingerprints on my neck for days. That was too much. The village pastor, Johannes Stecher, advised us to report the incident. I was to go to Naturns and get a medical certificate from Doctor Ferraro, an Italian doctor who had moved here. I borrowed a bike and rode there as advised. I showed the doctor my neck and only mentioned that someone had grabbed me by the throat, but not the name of the perpetrator. Ferraro wrote me a confirmation of my injury without any problem. Both incidents with Dalla Mariga were documented, the medical certificate enclosed, and the report sent to the relevant office in Bozen.

Weeks later we learned that the person having charges pressed against him was to be transferred. Dalla Mariga then came to my family personally to supplicate. His wife was a teacher in Karthaus, he himself had a senior position: they would be losing a lot with a punitive transfer, he argued. As compensation he therefore offered my father a job for my sister Luise as a domestic help. Father agreed, it was a good solution for all concerned. Dalla Mariga kept his word. Luise was properly treated and paid, he was allowed to stay, and he also treated me courteously when I later had to attend the *corso premilitare*, the military pre-service course.

We had come to an arrangement with the local fascist boss, but we could do nothing against the general fascist legislation. Sugar, matches and other 'luxury items' were subject to state monopoly and were therefore expensive and not affordable for our family. My mother made coffee from acorns, for example, and we had no sugar at all. Therefore we tried to get saccharine, although this sweetener was forbidden and possession of it was liable to prosecution. My father bought three of the coveted boxes from a smuggler, which contained the saccharin in the form of small tablets with 200 in each. Unfortunately, the joy of owning them did not last long. To explain why, I have to go back a little. At the end of the valley near Vernagt, where the reservoir is today, there was a place called *Piezet*. There was a small barn there. The Italian tax officials stayed overnight in them in their sleeping bags when they were carrying out their patrols and inspections at the far end of the valley. Now they got an extremely unpleasant surprise when they returned from one inspection. Somebody had used their absence to leave excrement in their sleeping bags. A warning, no doubt.

On that day, of all days, my father, who was on his way home with the saccharine in his jacket pocket, ran into the 'taxers'. He was immediately checked and they found the three forbidden boxes. The sentence was extremely severe. The saccharin was confiscated and he had to pay the value of two pairs of shoes as a fine. That was a lot of money at the time, especially for my father, who in any case had to gradually get back on his feet financially following the fire. At that time you had to cough up sixty days' wages for a pair of shoes! Such incidents were a topic of conversation that spread to the farthest corners of the valley and caused bitterness and hatred.

Chapter Four

Youthful exuberance

When I finished school, I could only just write the alphabet in Italian and my name. I wanted to learn to be a mechanic, but because a family misfortune intervened, my training could no longer be financed. My younger brother Peter, who helped my father in the small power station, got his foot caught in the wheels of a turbine and his leg was literally ripped off him. Seriously injured, he was carried on foot for a good 5 kilometres down the valley to Neuratheis Inn, as at that time the road into the Schnalstal only led up to as far as there. In addition, the telephone line from Neuratheis was only connected to a hotel at the entrance to the valley, so you had to organize a car this way. That was not easy either, as only very few people owned a car. Organizing the transport took a lot of time and, accordingly, my brother lost a huge amount of blood. The accident happened at nine in the morning and by three in the afternoon my brother was in the hospital in Meran/Merano, where at the last moment he was just saved from bleeding to death. His leg, however, had to be amputated because the machine had shredded the bones.

With only one leg my brother's chances of getting a decent job were very limited. So my father decided with foresight to enable Peter to train as a tailor. Peter successfully completed his apprenticeship and afterwards opened a tailor's shop in the Dorfmairhaus in Naturns.

After there was no longer any prospect for me of learning a trade, I worked as a day labourer with the farmers in the valley. And my craftsmanship too, which I had inherited from my father, brought me some small earnings: my talent was in demand with the farmers, especially when there was something to be repaired. I knew the inner workings of a pocket watch just as well as those of a padlock down to the last detail. I had no idea at that time that this knowledge would later save my life.

In addition to my work as a day labourer, I was also involved in the upgrading of the Schnalstal road. For many centuries the valley was only accessible over a footpath via Juval/Juvale, which was also used by pack animals. The first section of the road was opened in 1875 and initially only ran as far as Ratheis. In the following two years it was upgraded as far as Neuratheis. From here and with the help of pack animals and back-packs, goods were transported into the valley. In those days the only haulier in the valley was Serafin Gurschler from the Kurzhof in Kurzras/Maso Corto, and then his son Willi, who successfully continued on his legacy. From 1930 the road was gradually upgraded. In my youth, however, there was generally a lot of construction activity in the valley. Wherever I could I looked to be involved in order to earn something. This was also the case in 1933: with the field forge I had borrowed from my father I made the rock drills used for road construction on site.

The holes for blasting the rocks all had to be drilled by hand. Twenty people were engaged in this work alone. It took two men for each hole. One hit the masonry drill with a hammer while the other turned the drill. It happened one Saturday that the workers had failed to blast all the stones that had been prepared. Due to the fine weather no special precautions had been taken to cover the blast holes. So my friend Bernhard and I came up with the idea of filling the Sunday inactivity with a prank. We had watched the workers prepare the charges often enough, and then that Sunday afternoon we let all hell loose. More than ten charges exploded with a loud roar. Before the dust had settled we had already scarpered. We rushed to Unser Frau and mingled with the people to create an alibi for ourselves. On Monday there was a lot of speculation as to who the perpetrators were, but since there was no damage everyone soon returned to the usual work pattern. But we lads laughed for a long time at this prank.

When the work on the road construction stopped in autumn I went to Lana to pick apples. There I got to know Georg 'Jörg' Klotz, who would later be known to history as an activist for South Tyrol in the 1960s. He was a cheerful, amiable lad whom everyone liked a lot. During lunch there was often a fight. The watchword was: *Losst's amoll an Rumpler oi!* (Let's rumble!) Wrestling was a popular show of strength among the lads, but only for fun. With the money I got there as a harvest helper I was able to fulfil a great dream. I was passionate about going skiing with Bernhard, but I only had boards that I had crafted myself. Now I could buy myself real skis with bindings.

In 1934 and 1935 the fascists built barracks throughout the valley. Nobody knew the purpose of these buildings. Many years later I heard the rumour that the 30-metre-long barracks were to house prisoners of war. Once we discovered explosives in one of these barracks below Karthaus. The opening to let in light and air was just big enough to allow our narrow bodies to slip through. We stole kilos of explosive material and fuses. We messed around with it and had fun watching the potatoes fly through the air in the field. We even placed a small explosive charge into the so-called *Paterloch* of a family who lived in a renovated monastery cell and who were sitting having lunch. This was a device through which the food was passed during monastery times without the recipient being able to see the bearer. In the end not much happened apart from a bang. We had nothing against anyone in this family – only recklessness had driven us to this prank.

Another prank that I have never forgotten was also not without danger. We knew that Peter Grüner, in whose house the 'Fascist boss' lived with his wife, was not afraid to use his shotgun. It was strictly forbidden, but he owned a rifle with a detachable double barrel. When he left the house with it, the muzzle was hidden in his wide knickerbockers. So it was on one winter's day. There was enough snow on the ground, ideal for our prank. We met Peter 'by chance' and told him enthusiastically that we had tracked down a fox near a bridge. We also described to him where and how he could best find the animal. Then we parted; everything had gone as planned. In the meantime we put our stuffed fox, which was tied to a string, into position behind a gate. And Peter also took up position. To him it looked after all as if the animal had come down from the forest through the gap in the fence to stay in the meadow. At that moment he shot and hit it. Only this fox did not lie motionless but first disappeared behind a dung heap and then into the bushes that we dragged it into. Peter was greatly disappointed in not having hit it. And the second time too, because we repeated the prank. We lads of course were not aware of the dangers of the prank: it would not be the first time that someone would accidentally get shot.

Another experience from my youth happened in 1934. One day a gentleman came from Milan whose suitcase I was supposed to carry from Karthaus to the Kurzhof in Kurzras, which is about 10 kilometres. The suitcase was not particularly big, but was very heavy. When the gentleman saw that I could not carry the suitcase on my own, he grabbed it with me. When we arrived at our destination he bought me lunch at the Schwarzer Adler in Unser Frau. I did not know what it was, but it tasted very nice. When I described the food to my mother, she told me it was a schnitzel (Austrian meat cutlet). Thus I ate my first schnitzel at the age of 17!

Chapter Five

Germany sounded more promising

Until I was drafted into the Italian military I had not gone far beyond the Schnalstal: a couple of times to Meran, then to Lana to pick apples, by train to my military medical examination in Schlanders, and once by bicycle to Bozen. My best friend Bernhard Grüner studied there. You have to imagine it: I had barely turned 18 when I went to a cinema for the first time, in Bozen. It was an amazing experience for me.

Before I got my call-up, however, I had to complete the *corso premilitare* (military pre-service course). The training took place below Karthaus by the stream, where today the road to Oberpifrail leads. For several months in 1936 and 1937 I made a pilgrimage down there every Saturday to march, drill or get to know the individual weapons. However, we did not complete any shooting exercises.

On 15 March 1938 – Hitler had just marched into Austria – I was called up to the Italian army in Bassano del Grappa. From now on I was part of the 11th *Alpini* regiment, the Italian mountain troops. Around 240 of us South Tyrolers were billeted in the Barolini barracks; the rest of the regiment consisted of as many Italians.

Already on the first day I realized that it was every man for himself here. In the morning I went to the washrooms, screwed my razor together, put it on the sink, and soaped myself up. When I reached to get it again, it was already gone. That was a lesson for me. In order to prevent future losses I used an ink pen to mark my things with a Roman numeral 'twelve' where nobody could see it. But even marking my belongings did not prevent them from being stolen. In the gym we had to take off our hats for the exercises, among other things. When I had finished my programme and wanted to get my hat, I found a military type one instead of my own. After I had inspected the other hats and found my own, I waited for the thief and confronted him. But my Italian colleague acted up and said indignantly: '*Andiamo dal tenente!*,' 'Let's go to the lieutenant!' I agreed. There he

The recruits from Schnals deemed suitable for military service at their medical examination. Luis Raffeiner is lying on the right. Schlanders/Silandro, 19 June 1937.

complained vociferously. I explained to the lieutenant that I had marked all my belongings and showed him examples on my clothes. Then I turned the hat band of the object of dispute inside out, which also had a twelve drawn on it. The guy who had just been so insolent now turned pale and was punished. I got my things back that way from time to time. But I was also forced to use other methods. There was a pair of trousers for going out, which we called *Brandenhose*. *Branda* was the Italian name for the iron bed frame in our dormitory, which had a blanket and a woollen mattress on it. The leisure trousers were placed between the blanket and the mattress, then they were nicely 'ironed' when required. When I woke up one morning, the blanket was cut open and my trousers were gone. The thief had tampered under my bed that night. I was surprised at such audacity. I put on my blue overalls and went to the workshop to see my colleague Luis Schiefer from the Passeiertal. I told him about my loss and asked for help. I needed another pair of trousers urgently, as I couldn't go out in the evenings in my overalls!

There was a well in the barracks yard where everyone could wash their clothes. The soldiers sat in a corner by the clothesline and watched their belongings until they were dry. Our plan was as follows: while Luis started an argument when washing at the well, I would grab a suitable pair of

Raffeiner joined the *Alpini*, the Italian mountain infantry, pictured here marching on Monte Grappa in the province of Vicenza, 27 May 1938.

Comrades from the Vinschgau in the Barolini barracks in Bassano del Grappa. Raffeiner is second from the right in the second row. July 1939.

trousers from the clothes-line at the right moment. It worked wonderfully. So I got a pair of going-out trousers again. I was not proud of this method of reacquisition. But I didn't have much of a choice, since otherwise I would have had to pay for the trousers or the amount would have been deducted from my pay.

At the beginning of December 1938 I arrived in Terni near Rome, where I completed a weapons' master course. Things were also stolen here, as one day my mattress was gone. As a precautionary measure I had immediately marked my things and found my mattress again. Otherwise it was an interesting time, and our superiors always treated us well. We then went into the Dolomites for the winter manoeuvres in Asiago. We got skis and, along with the training, we also had a lot of fun. It was also not so strict here either. There was even a regimental race, which I did very well in. I also like to remember another incident there. A pal from the Schnalstal was also with us in Asiago. One day we ran into the *Taufenmacher*: they were craftsmen who made barrels and buckets from larch wood. These craftsmen from Asiago had been fetching wood from the Schnalstal in summer for several generations because the larches there were of excellent quality. After the trees were felled the wood was processed on the spot and tied into bundles, so-called *Taufenbinggl*, so that the mules could transport them. We knew these *Taufenmacher*, of course, and we were all very happy to meet each other again. My colleague from Schnals and I were invited to join them and spent many wonderful hours with these families during the winter manoeuvres.

During Pentecost in 1939 I was allowed to go home on holiday. When I got there I met Bernhard Grüner again. Bernhard and I had already gone to school together, and over the years a deep friendship had developed. We went into the mountains together, spent a lot of time together and hid no secrets from each other. His father was the postmaster in Schnals, and Bernhard studied in Bozen in the House of the Teutonic Order. At that time students were deliberately and primarily chosen for their political interests. It must have been the same with Bernhard, because he invited me to go to a mountain pasture with him. It would be really fun there, he promised me. We borrowed bicycles in Naturns and cycled to the next village but one, to Rabland/Rablà. At the Strasserhof Bernhard whistled for a young boy to join us, and then the three of us went on to the Tablander Alm above Partschins/Parcines. People came together there

Summer manoeuvres in the Dolomites, descending from the Marmolata glacier. 18 August 1939.

from all directions. There must have been about forty men and boys. There was a strange mood in the air, and a suspicion was gradually rising in me. It was a secret meeting, and it was about Hitler and National Socialism. There were drills and songs were sung: 'We want to march singing | into the new era | Adolf Hitler shall lead us | we are ready to fight.' For me it was the first time that I had come into close contact with National Socialist thinking and sympathies. The whole thing seemed strange to me, it was a real eye-opener. But then it was also quite funny and convivial, and so I thought no more about it.

After my holiday I returned to Bassano. We spent the summer in the Dolomites. At the end of August the captain got us to line up and said that he was very pleased with us and that we should not let ourselves be disturbed by the rumours that were circulating. There was not only speculation about the outbreak of war – Germany then effectively invaded Poland on 1 September 1939 – but also mainly about the future of us South Tyrolers. For some time we had been receiving news through the newspapers and through private contacts about a possible relocation of the German-speaking South Tyrolers to Germany, which had to be settled.

Sunday entertainment during the summer manoeuvres near Agordo in the province of Belluno. Luis Raffeiner is to the right of the accordion player. August 1939.

Luis Raffeiner (left) with comrades in front of the memorial for the fallen in Bassano del Grappa. Summer 1939.

In September 1939 all South Tyrolers were given leave from the military and sent home to discuss the so-called 'Option' with their families. I drove with great excitement to Karthaus to find out what was actually going on. At home I now knew for sure: we could decide in favour of Germanness, which meant emigrating to Germany. If you decided to remain, it meant the total abandonment of your own culture and language, as well as emigration from the homeland with settlement somewhere south of the river Po – at least those were the rumours.

My friend Bernhard was with the VKS, the *Völkischer Kampfring Südtirols*, which wanted to win over the population of South Tyrol for the option for Germany with a massive wave of propaganda. Bernhard worked on me too when I was home for the 'Option' decision. I was already 22 and could decide my own fate. He also instructed me to campaign for emigration among my relatives. When I actually spoke to a relative in Naturns about it, he raised his voice and overpowered me with a forceful torrent of words. Before I could say anything I heard him grumble that I should leave him alone and get lost. Then he left me standing there and walked away. He had decided to remain, and he would not be moved on the subject. The people's emotions were building up indescribably. During these times I experienced an unmitigated shambles: families, friends and neighbours fell out, cursing each other as traitors to the homeland and fascists. Our pastor from Karthaus spoke out in favour of staying. He was very cautious in his argument, but all the more resolutely he gave the impression that staying was the right decision. Unfortunately he was only a voice in the wilderness with his plea in the village, because the voices of those who were blinded by an ideology that corresponded more to wishful thinking than to reality were louder. I did not know this at the time, unfortunately. My family had voted for Germany without exception. Like most other ordinary folk, we gravitated towards the decision of educated people and those who were better off in the village, as well as our circle of friends. We trusted that they were properly informed and would not give up land and property so easily.

I myself had nothing to lose at home because I did not own anything and had no job – things could actually only get better. I felt more connected to Germany because of the language and culture – and also my hopes for a better future were linked to this. One or two propaganda slogans had certainly left their mark in the back of my mind, but my decision was mainly based on the emotional level. Germany sounded more promising than Sicily, and I knew only too well what to expect from fascism.

After the ten-day holiday I returned to Bassano. Of the 240 South Tyrolean soldiers in Bassano, only three had voted to stay, all the others had voted for Germany. The three 'remainers' were stigmatized and ridiculed as know-it-alls by the others. On 10 November 1939 we were released from the army. We got a discharge letter, the so-called *congedo*, and were allowed to go home. The soldiers were released in several stages, each time only forty South Tyrolers. It was feared that there could otherwise have been riots. On the way to Bozen things then became really boisterous: the *Heil Hitler!* alternated with German songs, and there was also drinking.

I took part, to be sure, but all in context. I was no fanatic anyway, but I did not want to completely cut myself off either. Right down the middle: I did not want to be among the first, and the dogs bite whoever is last, that was my motto. The alcohol did its job, the yelling from the open windows grew louder and louder and was too provocative for the Italian railway police. When we got out the railway guard ordered us to stand and step forward in rows of three in the waiting room. Then the *congedo* was taken from everyone again so that the details could be recorded. I did not like that at all. When it was our group's turn to step forward I watched the process closely. First the letter was taken from those in the front row, and when it was my turn, the second row, I slipped unnoticed into the first. Thus I saved my discharge letter, and holding on to it then made my return option – i.e. regaining Italian citizenship – much easier after the war had ended.

Chapter Six

Warm greetings from Gauleiter Hofer

On 8 December 1939 I was drafted into the German army, signed by SS-Sturmbannführer Dr Luig. I had to report at the Hotel Bristol in Bozen, the Official German Immigration and Remigration Office (*Amtliche Deutsche Ein- und Rückwanderungsstelle*) was located there.[4] When we were travelling by train towards the Brenner Pass soon after, white sheets were blowing in the wind as a farewell up as far as the highest farmyards. It was extraordinary, this departure from the homeland. There was a happy mood. The people waved, the sheets fluttered, the heart eagerly awaited the unknown adventure. I was happy to be leaving. I had the feeling of a new start that would bring with it new and maybe good things. On being transferred to the German Wehrmacht we soldiers became the first 'optants' of South Tyrol, who had already left our homeland in 1939. Also with us was my brother Toni, who had also been drafted and who was now travelling to Innsbruck with me.

When we arrived in Innsbruck, we were billeted in private houses, a few of us in the suburb of Igls. During a trip around the village a car with a Gauleiter's pennant stopped next to us. The window was wound down, and we greeted the occupants with a *Heil Hitler!* The passenger recognized us as South Tyrolers and asked when we had arrived. The man then gave us 20 marks, and said we should go to the Grünwalderhof Inn, have a beer there, and give them warm greetings from Gauleiter Hofer. We got our beer and gave them the message, but we still did not know who this Gauleiter Hofer was.

On 20 December we arrived at the Jesuit monastery in Innsbruck; there we were quartered and at the same time received our German citizenship with the official certificate of naturalization. The monks had been driven out of the monastery. As I walked into the courtyard of the monastery I

Amtliche Deutsche
Ein-und Rückwandererstelle
Hauptstelle

Bozen,den 8.Dezember 1939.
Hotel Bristol

Herrn

Raffeiner

SIE HABEN WÄHREND DER FAHRT JEG-·
LICHES SINGEN UND GRÖHLEN ZU UNTER-
LASSEN!
BEACHTEN SIE DIE GESETZE DES LANDES!

A n w e i s u n g .

        Auf Grund der Besprechungen zwischen Berlin und Rom
sind Sie aus dem italienischem Heer entlassen worden,um in die
Deutsche Wehrmacht überführt zu werden.
        Sie fahren nun am Samstag den 16.Dezember mit den fahr-
planmässigen Zuge,der am Brenner um 10.20 Uhr eintrifft nach
Innsbruck,um dort in die Deutsche Wehrmacht überführt zu werden.
Mitzubringen haben Sie :
        Italien. Mod. 4,soweit bereits erhalten
        2 Lichtbilder
        Kamm und Haarbürste
        Rasierzeug und Rasierseife
        Waschseife
        Kleiderbürste
        3 Kleiderbügel
        Stiefelwichse und Schuhbürste
        Taschentücher
        Unterzeug,soweit vorhanden.
Sonstiges Gepäck ist nur mitzunehmen,wenn Sie Bekannte oder Ver-
wandte in Innsbruck haben,bei denen Sie das Gepäck abstellen kön-
nen.
        Ihr Grenzübertritt erfolgt auf Grund eines Sammelpasses,
der bei der italienischen und bei der Deutschen Grenzpolizei am
Brenner aufliegt.- Die Fahrkarte von Ihrem Abfahrtsorte (Bahnsta-
tion)bis Brenner erhalten Sie in der Anlage;diese Fahrkarte ist
von Ihnen vor Abfahrt des Zuges am Fahrkartenschalter vorzulegen,
wo Sie vom Schalterbeamten ausgefüllt wird.Die Fahrkarte Brenner-
Innsbruck erhalten Sie am Brenner ausgehändigt.
        Sie können einen Betrag bis zu Lire 240.- (nur in 10-
Lirescheinen) mitnehmen,der Ihnen in Innsbruck zu RM.50.- umge-
wechselt wird.

                        Der Leiter der Hauptstelle :

                              gez.Dr. Luig

                        ⅜ - Sturmbannführer.

Luis Raffeiner opted to emigrate to Germany, which is why he was released from the Italian army and transferred to the Wehrmacht. With this document he travelled to Innsbruck on 16 December 1939.

Deutsches Reich

Einbürgerungsurkunde

Alois Raffeiner

in   Innsbruck, Jesuitenkloster

geboren am   23.7.1917   in   Kartaus

hat mit dem Zeitpunkt der Aushändigung dieser Urkunde die deutsche Staatsangehörigkeit (Reichsangehörigkeit) durch Einbürgerung erworben.

Die Einbürgerung erstreckt sich nicht auf Familienangehörige.

Innsbruck, den   20. Dez.   19 39

Der Landeshauptmann von Tirol:

Im Auftrag:

(Dr. Pfenner)

Gebührenfrei.
Kennziffer: 704.062.
Anschlußziffer:

With this document dated 20 December 1939 Raffeiner obtained German citizenship.

Luis Raffeiner (centre) with his brother Toni (left) and another South Tyroler on their arrival in Igls (Austria). All three have a swastika on their lapel. December 1939.

saw how a mountain of prayer books and scriptures had been burned. That was when the light went on in my head for the first time. I remembered the rumours I had heard at home in fragments from a 'remainer' organization. Some of them actually knew more than the broad masses, to which I too belonged. Then at Christmas I also came to understand that there was something against the Church. On Christmas Eve we were forbidden to go to mass. Instead, there was a Christmas party in the large town hall in Innsbruck at which Gauleiter Franz Hofer and other Nazi personalities slung around powerfully eloquent speeches. Above all, the SS was promoted, the 'protection squad' of the Nazi Party. There was plenty of good food and drink, and the atmosphere in the hall was wonderful. That evening, many South Tyrolers registered for the SS. I too was pushed: I was told that I was a strapping chap and should register. I said, however, that I would not be suitable and would prefer the Wehrmacht. I simply felt uneasy about the enthusiasm with which the SS was promoted. The fact that we were forbidden to go to Christmas mass and the burning of the books in the Jesuit monastery were the decisive warning signals for me. I knew some decent lads who had got carried away. There were some fanatics from the South Tyrolean lowlands who shouted *Heil Hitler* to the point of hoarseness out of enthusiasm or perhaps even under

Nazi Christmas party in the large town hall in Innsbruck with Gauleiter (local Party leader) Franz Hofer. 24 December 1939.

the influence of alcohol and did not have the faintest idea what they were getting themselves into. There was no turning back any more.

My brother Toni was released from military service because he had a chronic condition. For me it had already started on Boxing Day: we had to march in double-time to Hall. From there we were moved in the New Year to the Scherzhauserfeldsiedlung in Salzburg. Here the general said in his address: 'We are pleased that you have volunteered for the German Wehrmacht!' 'Well, bravo!', I thought to myself. You could also see it that way. What would have happened if I had voluntarily had no desire for either the German or the Italian military?

We were then dressed in military clothing, and I began my three-month training with the mountain troops of the 137th Regiment. We were not allowed to go out for a whole month. We were properly drilled: 'Lie down, get up, march, march, gas mask on, a song!' was what we heard the whole time. It was indescribable. At the end of the training in February 1940 I even got a hernia during this grind and was taken to the Sankt Josef Hospital in Salzburg. Not only was my hernia treated there but I also got my appendix removed. There were other South Tyrolers in the hospital, even a Naturnser, 'Latschraun Sepp'. We were a funny group. The

Comrades in the Scherzhauserfeldsiedlung barrack camp. Salzburg, early 1940.

War as a game. Training to be a *Gebirgsjäger* (mountain infantryman) in Salzburg.

attending doctor, Dr Mitterstiller from Innsbruck, took a real shine to us and tried to keep us in the hospital as long as possible. To do this, he specifically made up the existence of an epidemic that had broken out and even had the walls repainted as a consequence. After I had been released from the hospital in Salzburg, I spent the time from 7 May to 4 June in the convalescent home in Ehrwald in Tyrol. Then I had to go straight to my unit, which was in the barracks in Lehen. It was already afternoon by the time I had packed up, done the paperwork and was back in the barracks. When I arrived at the barracks it seemed deserted. No one was to be seen. I went to the upper rooms where the dormitory was and looked out from the corridor onto the courtyard. They were all lined up in rank and file down there, and I kept hearing 'I swear!' being shouted. The swearing-in was taking place and I had arrived too late. How should I act now? I could not just burst in now. I decided to hide in the toilet. When everyone came up, I just mixed in with them all. So nobody knew exactly whether I had been there or not. The next day the unit started to head for Norway. They did not take me with them because the formalities were not yet done for me. Thus I ended up back in a recruit company. I also had to do training

Raffeiner in sports attire. Salzburg, summer 1940.

During his time in the Hellbrunn and Glasenbach barracks, Raffeiner (standing, foreground left) was assigned to look after the horses.

After the hay harvest with farmers in the Salzburg region. Luis Raffeiner is on the far right. Summer 1940.

for a second time at the Hellbrunn and Glasenbach barracks. Here I had a South Tyrol colleague as an instructor: I had already met Anton Staffler from Lana in Bassano del Grappa. Now he was my instructor here every now and then, which was a relief for me because I was allowed to rest in the bushes once in a while when he was in charge. Otherwise, we recruits had to bravely struggle through the mud in the fields around Lehen.

In the autumn of 1940 I was given leave. First, I was faced with the question: where to go? I had a cousin near Innsbruck, but I was hoping for more prospects of work at my sister's in Karlsruhe. My sister Luise had also opted for Germany and had come to Karlsruhe in April 1940 with sixteen other women from South Tyrol to train as a midwife in the clinic. I visited my sister and then went to the employment office. There, a woman from Alsace gave me the address of the Bauersfeld company in the neighbouring town of Heidelberg, which specialized in the manufacture of machines and equipment and was looking for workers. The fate of the South Tyrolers did not fail to affect this woman because she had had a similar experience. I had not learned a trade, but I was interested in technology and therefore very excited about this work. I introduced myself there as a South Tyroler who had emigrated and was on work leave and also said that I only had my uniform. Mr Bauersfeld, the owner of the company, was a very nice man. He said he had heard about the South Tyrol 'option' and would be glad to have me. Then he took me by the arm, led me into his bedroom, opened the wardrobe and took out one of his tightest pairs of trousers – the gentleman was a little more corpulent than me – a blue jacket and a belt and pressed the things into my arms. He also found me a place to live with a nice family near the company. The next day he showed me my workplace, where about twelve workers were busy manufacturing automatic meat grinders and sausage-filling machines. The clients were butchers, but everything was produced for the Wehrmacht. I liked the job and as a beginner I did not need to feel ashamed. I watched the others closely and learned quickly, so that they were very happy with me.

After a few days a worker – his name was Siefermann – came up to me and asked me if I wanted to smoke a cigarette. 'Thank you,' I replied, 'but smoking is not allowed in the workplace.' The next day, when I was working in the forge, the same man came up to me again and invited me to go with him to the Goldener Knopf Inn on Adolf-Hitler-Platz on

Raffeiner and his sister Luise visiting the family of Siefermann, the foreman of the Bauersfeld company, during his working holiday. Karlsruhe, October 1940.

Luise Raffeiner with friends and women from the *Winterhilfswerk* (Winter Relief Organization), who are collecting donations for the war. Karlsruhe, winter 1940/1941.

Saturday. I said yes. On Saturday we first met at his apartment and then went to the aforementioned pub together. At the time there was a blackout everywhere in Germany: no light was allowed to shine onto the street, and the street lights were turned off. There were constant patrols. Whenever light came out somewhere from even a small crack, somebody would knock on the window and vigorously shout in the command *Verdunkeln!* (Blackout!) The reason for this was that everything had to be dark so that the British could not easily locate the cities with their aeroplanes. When we arrived at the inn, there was already quite a lot of fun being had at some of the tables. It was a nice evening. *Polizeistunde* (police hour) was at 11pm. The room emptied, most people leaving the inn through the front door. We disappeared through another door and found ourselves in an adjoining room where there were about thirty people. The windows were completely covered, and things were really getting going here. The conversation level increased, people made fun of Adolf Hitler, and there was an anti-Nazi mood. As a South Tyroler, I was fêted. But the whole thing made me feel very uncomfortable. My companion noticed this and calmed me down: I had no need to worry, he said, there were even high-ranking police officers among the guests, and those present were all opponents of Hitler. The situation was watertight, he added. Here I saw that behind the façade some things looked very different.

My companion that evening was appointed foreman in the company a short time later; his predecessor, a die-hard Nazi, was disgusted. The farewell from the company was very hospitable when in March 1941 I was called up once again to the barracks in Lehen in Salzburg. I returned once again to the recruit unit and continued my *Gebirgsjäger* training. Needless to say I did not jump for joy. I was gradually getting sick of the whole thing.

Chapter Seven

Training as a tank mechanic

During shooting exercises in April 1941 the *Spieß* (first sergeant) came and called out loudly: 'Raffeiner!' I stepped forward to him and waited for his instructions. He asked: 'You're a mechanic?' 'Yes!' I answered. 'Come to my office at lunchtime today!' I was curious to know what awaited me. At noon in the office, the first sergeant cleared things up for me. 'I'm telling you something, but please keep it to yourself!' were his first emphatic words. 'It's about a technical unit.' Technical unit – that was music to my ears. I was interested in everything that had to do with technology. He was talking about 24-ton tanks belonging to a special unit, so-called *Sturm-geschützpanzer* (assault guns), which had been successfully tested in the French campaign in the summer of 1940. 'These tanks are a secret weapon and are supposed to break through towards the enemy in conjunction with the infantry,' the first sergeant continued. He also explained to me that each battery would consist of seven such tanks, and the entire unit would comprise 500 men. 'Mechanics are needed to maintain these tanks,' he finally summed up. If I wanted, I could do a tank mechanic training course in the Adolf-Hitler-Lager in Jüterbog near Berlin. Finally, he again referred to the strict secrecy of the project and gave me time to decide. That did not take me long. After eight days I got the news: 'You have to leave at one o'clock tonight, Raffeiner!' I took the train to Berlin. The first sergeant warned me that I should not miss the stop at the third station after the small town of Wittenberg. 'Otherwise it'll turn out badly for you' were his words. That sounded mysterious, almost frightening. So I paid close attention and got off at the third station. It was a deserted area, pine forest all around and only a small sentry box. A sentry was standing there and asked for my papers. 'Fine, continue along the road,' he said. I marched off and after about ten minutes I met a soldier. I greeted him and asked: 'Comrade, how does it look in there?' The man patted me on the shoulder and said: 'Comrade, go back to where you came from, all hell has broken out in there!'

What had I got myself into? But it was too late to back down now. The first thing I got to see were recruits who were being hounded through the area with the command 'Lie down, get up, march, march!' That sounded very familiar to me. Then I came to the camp and reported for duty as I had been told. The next morning the training already started, but first of all an hour of 'footwork' was announced, during which a problem arose for me already. Our instructor was a Prussian, and I did not understand him, at least not properly. Since I had to follow what the others were doing, I was always too late responding to the orders. You can imagine what that looked like. At any rate the instructor was not best pleased with me. Once he yelled at me: 'Crawl!' I lay down immediately and crawled a little until the next order came. Unfortunately I misunderstood this and continued crawling until someone came running after me and shouted: 'Raffeiner, you have to go back!'

My comrades then cleared the matter up. They told the instructor that I was a Tyroler and that I would often not understand him properly. From

Training as an assault-gun attendant in the Adolf-Hitler-Lager in Jüterbog near Berlin. April 1941.

The soldiers had no idea where their deployment would lead them.

then on the superior was very friendly to me and almost apologetically said that he had not known this. After the daily physical exercise in the morning, we – about 30 men – had technical lessons. An engineer in civilian clothes explained to us all the technical intricacies of a tank and explained to us what to do in case of a breakdown. The lessons were really very interesting. There was also a comrade with us who gained everyone's attention in his own unique way. It is difficult to explain, but very many of us were unnerved by the almost meticulous attention with which he followed the class. He was called Michael Scheurer, but we also called him *Kittelprunzer* (robe soiler) because he had come here from the Bavarian monastery in Ansbach. One day he was the victim of a prank: during a class a recruit secretly stuck the tube of a grease pump into his pocket, and another guy then started to pump. The trouser pocket got ever bigger and was already bulging considerably. Meanwhile, others also noticed the prank. Michael Scheurer was listening to the lesson as always with motionless attention when he suddenly winced and put his hand into his trouser pocket. Everyone laughed. Scheurer then raised his hand and snitched on the unknown perpetrators.

'Who was that?' the instructor asked the class. General silence. He continued with the lesson but kept asking about the culprit. Again and again there was collective silence. 'For the last time, who was it?' No answer.

'So, then, fall in!' the commanding officer finally ordered. Then followed an indescribably tough drill. We had to exercise so hard that our tongues could only hang out: 'Lie down, up, march, gas mask on, a song!' It was pure torture. The man on the receiving end of the joke was not spared, he too had to participate. The motto was: 'One for all and all for one!' At five o'clock in the morning the drill continued. We had to pay for the prank for a whole week, we were really beaten up. After these eight days we were again asked who it was. But this time too there was only silence. 'So, now I have seen that you are soldiers: one for all and all for one!' That was the end of the matter.

A short time later my training was over: I graduated as one of the best in my class and from then on was responsible for the technical maintenance of assault guns. At the time, however, I did not know what exactly was in store for me.

It was the end of April 1941 when the situation in the camp suddenly changed. Assault-gun units were assembled and left the camp overnight.

It was our turn too. Our destination was Treuenbrietzen, which lies between Jüterbog and Berlin. Our *Sturmgeschützabteilung* 243 consisted of three batteries with seven tanks each. The detachment consisted of about 500 men: drivers, replacements, mechanics, and kitchen staff. I had been assigned to the second battery as a tank mechanic; it had the field-post number 36814.

When we arrived in Treuenbrietzen the entire assault-gun detachment including the twenty-one tanks was presented on the town square to demonstrate the power and strength of Germany to the population. It was the first and last time that we appeared like this as a cohesive detachment. Later, in the Russian campaign, each battery was more or less on its own and repeatedly assigned to other army units. Depending on the specific order, we were used for different missions. We were regarded as a kind of suicide squad. We then spent a week in this small town, after which our unit was loaded onto the railway and headed for Poland.

Officers of the second battery of the *Sturmgeschützabteilung* 243 (assault-gun detachment 243): Lieutenant Causemann, Lieutenant Günter Gerlitz, First Lieutenant Friedrich Malzan, Lieutenant Jesch. Jüterbog, April/May 1941.

Until now my time as a soldier had been quite exhausting at times, but nothing really alarming had happened. But now we knew: things were getting serious. There was a rumour that we were going to Iraq to attack the British in the rear. It was said that the Russians would let us through. When we arrived in Rzeszów in Poland we were unloaded and continued on along the road. Tiredness spread: a tank driver fell asleep and flattened a telegraph pole. After that we spent the night in a forest. We were not informed of our destination. We only knew now that the Iraq thing could not be right.

As we were driving through a never-ending forest to Rzeszów, we were presented with a picture we had never seen before. The whole forest was teeming with soldiers and military units. Infantry, artillery and engineer units with their pontoons were hidden in the forest. Pontoons were used as floating platforms for crossing rivers if there were no bridges. I remembered that I had seen them on the river Salzach during my training in Salzburg. When we had crossed the forest and were back driving in the

'Sir, please, bread.' On the way to the Eastern Front by train. Poland, June 1941.

Raffeiner's assault-gun unit after unloading at the train station in Rzeszów the day before the attack on the Soviet Union. Poland, 21 June 1941.

open we soon reached Zamość. There was a sign there that read: 'Can be seen by the enemy.'

Now we learned that Russia was our objective. At this point the name 'Operation Barbarossa' was mentioned for the first time. We could not have imagined anything like this at all. In any case we simple soldiers were not given any further information. And nobody would have dared to ask. Nobody at all dared to discuss political decisions, not even among their closest circle of comrades. We then drove on to Bełżec; we were about 3 kilometres away from the Russian border.

Our unit was split up and sent into different positions. I saw the local population digging trenches everywhere; something was in the air. That night we heard a speech by Hitler on the radio: he was spouting something about the Bolshevik danger and the salvation of the whole of European civilization and culture. At the end of the speech the Antichrist Hitler even asked for divine assistance in this difficult struggle.

Chapter Eight

Crimes against humanity

It was shortly after two o'clock in the morning on 22 June 1941 when the order came for my battery to mount – the Russian campaign had begun. From Bełżec we went towards the border. As a tank mechanic – I had the rank of private – I had to go with the combat unit. We were part of Army Group South. Since there was only room for four men in the tank, I had made standing room for myself with a board on the back of the tank. Only when things got really dangerous would they bring me inside regardless. But not on that night.

Thus began the war up close and personal for me too. To my left and right, on either side the tanks, the infantry advanced. I was told to shoot my machine gun from my position. But I did not do this because I saw my duty primarily as a technician. Above all, however, I did not want to shoot anyone – I might be called a coward – and prayed that no one would shoot me either. A tank was probably powerful enough itself, what could I stop with a machine gun?

There was already a loud crash along the whole front. An indescribably terrible inferno arose – there was howling and booming everywhere. We heard the 'Big Berta', the legendary cannon from the First World War, which was standing on railway tracks about a kilometre away from us. This gun was so incredibly and deafeningly loud that it made me feel truly miserable. I stood on the back of the tank and sent prayers heaven-bound. During these hours there was a throng of war that simply cannot be described. At seven in the morning we had the first dead comrade to mourn. For the first time I experienced war in its brutal and cruel reality. It was a night of hell.

We had attacked the Russians without a prior declaration of war. After crossing the border we approached a line of Russian bunkers. While the infantry advanced with five tanks from our battery, we had to stay back with two tanks and keep the enemy artillery in check: the Russians had

The grave of the first dead soldier of *Sturmgeschützabteilung* 243 near Bełżec on the then Polish-Russian border. Poland, 22 June 1941.

entrenched themselves in three-storey bunkers and were firing at us with their artillery guns. Our assault guns were so accurate that we could aim directly into the embrasures of the bunkers from a distance of about one and a half kilometres. Nevertheless, the engagement lasted for two days; on the third day the survivors hung white sheets from the bunkers as a sign of surrender. Captivity awaited them. We had used grenades with a percussion fuse, which meant that they only exploded inside the building. How it looked in there afterwards was horrible. Some comrades had gone into the bunkers and told us about it.

After this mission we followed after our unit. The road led us first to Rava-Ruska, lying just across the Polish border in modern-day Ukraine, where we stayed overnight. In Nemirov, our next stop about 20 kilometres away, we provided entertainment for the local population. One of the soldiers had got hold of a gramophone from somewhere and played Russian records for the villagers. We generally spent many a happy hour with the Russian rural population during our advance.[5] We met women, children and old people in the villages. They mostly lived in miserable

A Bunker between Rava-Ruska and Nemirov captured by Raffeiner's unit. Ukraine, June 1941.

Downed Russian plane at Rata near Rava-Ruska. Summer 1941.

wooden huts. Everything that nature and the surrounding area provided had been used to build these huts: intertwined branches as walls, a mixture of animal dung and clay as filler material and a kind of lime as plaster. They had no beds, though they did not sleep on the bare clay floor but mostly on straw or on brick-built wood stoves, but it was not comfortable.

I also had a kind of little Russian dictionary in my kit, which we had been given shortly after crossing the Russian border. I diligently studied the most important Russian terms in it that could be useful for us soldiers

'Stalin is captured, but only in the picture.' Raffeiner's caption on the back of the photo. Near Rava-Ruska, summer 1941.

'Tourist's view' of land and people. Nemirov, summer 1941.

German soldiers playing Russian records on a captured gramophone for the Ukrainian villagers. Near Nemirov, summer 1941.

Panzer lieutenant Günter Gerlitz with an NCO. Ukraine, summer 1941.

when dealing with the Russian population. You could therefore at least exchange a few words.

Back to our advance: from Nemirov we came to a small place that I remember as Mosliviltse. Here I saw for the first time how Jews were being treated. I had certainly heard of the events of the *Reichskristallnacht* (Night of the Broken Glass) in Germany at the end of 1938, but I had never experienced anything like that myself before.[6] Nor can I say there was any anti-Jewish sentiment within our assault-gun detachment, though we did lack any kind of political awareness anyway. Here in this place not far from the Polish-Russian border I now saw how the Jews – they were all men – had to build roads and were fiercely tormented by members of the Wehrmacht in the process. They looked pathetic. I could not do anything to change the situation; it was only in dealing with people on an individual level that it was possible for me to show a little humanity.

Comrades Franz Reichelt and Lothar Gladrow in a Ford; next to them is a man from the office and another comrade. On the front of the right fender can be seen the emblem of *Sturmgeschützabteilung* 243: the 'Iron Knight' with the identification mark of the respective battery: clubs, spades, hearts or diamonds.

Jews being harassed not far from the Polish-Russian border. Summer 1941.

The tanks were on a hill next to the church, and I had a Jew carry my tool-bag up. In exchange I gave him a loaf of bread. The expression of his gratitude went deep into my soul; it was an expression that struck me deeply.

After this stay we drove on eastwards via Tarnopol to Berdichev and then Zhitomir, a distance of around 500 kilometres altogether. We were right to the fore during the capture of these two towns. It must have been the beginning of July. This meant that we were operating in the third echelon behind the infantry and artillery and were firing over these two at enemy troops. Our guns were still very accurate even at a distance of 3 kilometres.

In Zhitomir I saw how a church service was held again after thirty years of abstinence. The people came to this event from far away. It may sound paradoxical, but for these people we were more liberators than aggressors.

Our next stop was Vinnitsa, south of Zhitomir. An SS unit was already there. From Vinnitsa we moved on to the nearby town of Bar. Apparently there was a GPU prison in this place, in which Russian prisoners – political opponents of communism – were detained.[7] We only found out about this days later after we had passed through this place. A German officer – I no longer know his rank or function – told us that hundreds of Russians had been massacred in this prison. As proof of this he showed us photos, which did indeed have corpses in them. When the photo was being taken, according to the officer, a woman was looking for her relative among the brutally murdered people. And one of the men was still alive – he lifted up his arms whimpering, his eyes had been gouged out. We believed at once that it had been a 'clean-up' operation by the SS. However, the officer emphasized that the Russians had got rid of their own political opponents here and wanted to blame the SS for the crime. In this way further hatred towards the German aggressors was to be stirred up among their own population. This rectification was important to the officer; for us it was definitely credible. We also learned that a mass grave with around 2,500 dead had been found in the underground part of this prison.

We would have gladly done without such images of horror. During our advance, however, we experienced and saw the excesses of violence every day: corpses of fallen Russians lying around by the roadside, hanged 'partisans' or Jews who were rounded up and then killed, we witnessed all this, of course. At some point, however, you become deadened to such

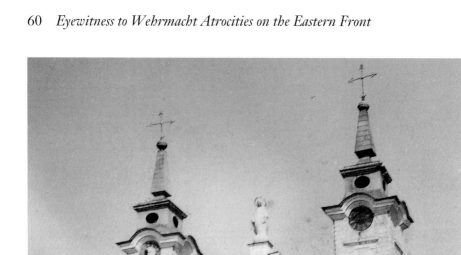

After thirty years of communism a church service could take place once again under the German occupation. Zhitomir, July 1941.

What do these pictures show? Massacred Russian political prisoners who were allegedly found in a prison run by the Soviet secret police, the GPU? The People's Commissariat of the Interior (NKVD) blamed the Germans for such massacres. German Propaganda Minister Joseph Goebbels in turn had photos of victims of NKVD atrocities distributed among the soldiers to demonstrate the inhumanity of the Russians. At the same time thousands of Jews were shot by the SS 'in retaliation'.

images and no longer consciously notice them. Nevertheless, I often also captured these terrible experiences with a camera. A cousin of mine, a staunch Nazi, had given me a Voigtländer camera as a present. As a functionary of the *Völkischer Kampfring Südtirols*, the Nazi organization in South Tyrol, he did not have to go to war for the moment. Therefore I was to record impressions of the war for him so that he could participate in it that way.

On our further advance eastwards we reached Gaisin and then the Uman metropolitan area; in the vicinity of this town the so-called *Kessel-schlacht* (encirclement battle) of Uman then took place at the beginning of August. Our armoured detachment was not directly involved in the fighting, but was only on the edge of the battle of encirclement. The Russians

Tanks of *Sturmgeschützabteilung* 243 on the advance, with burning houses in the background. Ukraine, summer 1941.

Destruction of a Russian tank during the advance.

'You took what you needed.' Soldiers and kitchen personnel with a slaughtered cow. Summer 1941.

Field kitchen with soldiers peeling potatoes. The soldiers had to 'organize' their own food, as there was no provision for supplies.

Inspecting a Russian 24-ton tank, captured during the advance. Summer 1941.

Death was a constant companion. Initially, the fallen were buried with crosses made beforehand. 2 July 1941.

were completely surrounded from all directions by our units. The battle lasted for a few days and many soldiers died on the battlefield. The number of prisoners was enormous.

After the *Kesselschlacht* at Uman the hinterland as far as the Black Sea and the river Dnieper was open to us for a wide-ranging advance. Our next objective was Kiev, where we were to give support to the capturing of the city. For that we had to cross the Dnieper. With our two assault guns we took the ferry across the river. During the crossing it was important that we were flanked by the infantry. They protected our sides because the thin side plates were the weak point of our tanks. I was scared as hell because I could not swim. Artillery fire crashed down beside us and there were planes constantly overhead. Thank God we crossed the river unscathed. The Russians received us over there at once. That night we were hemmed in. The Russians had broken through with their gunboats and were coming down the Dnieper. We were now subordinated to Panzer Group von Kleist commanded by the eponymous Colonel General Ewald von Kleist, which was currently in the middle of the encirclement battle at Kiev. Our two tanks were not far from where the Dnieper and the Desna rivers meet – in their wedge, so to speak. The river was widest here. Sometimes we did not know where the enemy was. Only at night could you

Resting at a typical Russian kolkhoz (collective farm) during the advance. Summer 1941.

A tank is 'ammunitioned', i.e. armed with shells.

Raffeiner's tank *Blondine* ('Blondie') is made ready for battle. Summer 1941.

During the advance the German soldiers mainly encountered women and children. Ukrainian folk festival, summer 1941.

see exactly where the front line was, because the enemy's flares were more reddish and duller than ours. Flares were used to better locate enemy territory at night and to make it visible. With our two tanks we found ourselves together with the infantry in the vanguard of the front once again. We encountered German troops and immediately had to fine-tune our guns so that we would not hit our own comrades. Kiev, in the meantime, was encircled in a wide salient through the forests. The battle for the city lasted more than a month: the way it looked after such turmoil due to combat was so macabre that it really sapped my nerves. In some cases you could no longer speak of corpses. Only fragments of humans were lying around; body parts were even hanging in the trees. Dismembered horses and smashed carts were also part of the horror scene. The number of Russian prisoners after the encirclement battle at Kiev was enormous: apparently there were around 650,000.

I had already seen the prisoners march from the Uman encirclement battle. This endless procession of three rows trudged past us for hours. They must have been already walking for days and they probably had not been given anything to eat. I was witness to an incident that I have not forgotten to this day. A dead horse lay by the road. It was midsummer, and the animal had been bloated by the gases created by the heat. Countless

After the encirclement battle at Kiev, a few days later. The telegraph connections, which are indispensable for the transmission of messages, have already been restored. August/September 1941.

The Battle of Kiev lasted more than a month and the ring around the city was littered with burned-out vehicles. The wounded and dead have already been taken away.

The endless wreckage was scoured for anything useful.

Captured Russians cleaning up after the encirclement battle at Kiev. September 1941. The number of Russian prisoners was enormous.

Prisoners in a seemingly endless procession. September 1941.

Inspecting a damaged tank after the encirclement battle at Kiev, September 1941.

flies, attracted by the stench of decay, were swarming around the carcass. Suddenly there was an explosive 'pffff': the horse had burst and its entrails flew out. A prisoner broke free from the column, rushed over to the horse, tugged at the stinking entrails, stuffed them greedily into his mouth, and then hastily fed the rest into his tin can. Then he rejoined the procession of prisoners. I felt sick to my stomach at this sight and a thought, a prayer, shot into my head: 'May God save us from such a fate!' Shortly after this episode another Russian prisoner broke from the column, and this time he came straight towards us. We were positioned on the roadside with our tanks, and the Russian begged for bread. One of the men in our detachment drew his pistol and pointed it at the prisoner, but he did not shoot because the Russian quickly rejoined the procession of prisoners.

Chapter Nine

In the Jewish ghetto

Due to my technical competence, I was called the 'tank doctor' within my unit, and I was sometimes 'borrowed' by other batteries, especially when it came to difficult work such as adjusting the support brakes and steering brakes. That was mostly anything but pleasant, because I often found myself in the middle of the artillery fire. Sometimes I thought to myself that only a miracle would get me out of this hell alive. But I was very happy that I was not forced to use weapons myself.

It was autumn, and after the operation around Kiev we drove northwards with our battery of *Sturmgeschützabteilung* 243 to Gomel in Belorussia and then on to the Russian town of Klintsy, a total of a good 300 kilometres. On the way, when we were stopped again in a village for

Tanks frequently got stuck in the mud. Locals and comrades watch. In the background can be seen a bombed-out church. Near Oster, Ukraine, September 1941.

Raffeiner's tank *Yorck* pictured in a stream, after the bridge failed to take the weight.

A German plane behind the front line. A general had been flown in for a briefing.

a rest, a colleague and I sought a place to sleep in a Russian woman's house. Suddenly we were roused from our slumber. 'Bombili, Bombili,' it sounded to us. The woman shouted excitedly and gestured with her arms. A petrol depot in the immediate vicinity had actually been bombed and had exploded. We had slept soundly and noticed nothing, the tiredness showed its effect. And this was not without danger. Our comrades had meanwhile brought the two tanks to safety during the bombing. Just at the last moment we saw it turn the corner, so we could still catch up with it.

From Klintsy we set out for Bryansk: the town was about 200 kilometres to the north-east and had been captured in mid-October. For a while there was not much to do for my Panzer Group there, also because we had no more tanks. What had happened? Fire had broken out in a hall in which my unit and the assault guns were camped. The flames had surprised us during the night, and only we could escape from the building. But all seven tanks exploded.

But once again I was chosen for a special assignment. Our lieutenant, whose name I have forgotten, had an expensive car that was dear to him.

Advancing from Kiev via Chernigov (Ukraine), Gomel (Belorussia) and Klintsy towards Bryansk (Russia), the Germans left a trail of devastation. September 1941.

A burning petrol depot bombed by the Russians. September 1941.

Now he wanted the vehicle to be overhauled. To do this we had to drive specially to a drilling and grinding workshop in Minsk. There were four of us: our lieutenant, an NCO named Seifenheld, a second motor mechanic and me. At the beginning of November we drove to Minsk in two cars and delivered both of them to the workshop. In Minsk there was an officers' quarters, and the lieutenant got out there, but we had to organize our own accommodation. In the typical manner of the conqueror we rumbled into some hut without first knocking. We were completely amazed when the housewife addressed us here on Russian soil in German. She told us that she was a Volga German. Her name was Gareis, she had a son and two daughters, and she told us how she had got here. We stayed with her and spent two weeks with the family.

There was a supply depot located in the lower rooms of the city's so-called Lenin House. There we could get our food with a ration ticket. Now, with the permission of our lieutenant, we wrote a one in front of the four. So we got food for fourteen people and also looked after the family we lived with as well as the Jews in the workshop who brought the car back into shape for us in the installation pit. They were happy to eat, did their job with great diligence, and we made ourselves comfortable.

We had a lot of fun with the two pretty girls in the family, but only in a friendly way. Our lieutenant was a decent chap and had warned us not to touch the nice girls. In the evenings we usually all sat together in front of the stove on the clay floor, and my fellow mechanic – his name was Spinke – acted like a comedian. He had talent: there was a lot to laugh about and we really had a fun time. We even went to the cinema. In view of the brutal combat experiences of the last few weeks, this cheerfulness did us good. On one of these evenings, Mrs Gareis also told us about a Jewish ghetto that was only a few hundred metres away from us. There would be a lot of useful items lying around in this camp, she explained to us, and asked if we could get her some bed frames from there. Like us, they slept on the cold floor, so we promised that we would have a look around.

This Jewish ghetto consisted of an entire district of Minsk, fenced off with barbed wire and guarded by machine-gun posts. Sergeant Seifenheld accompanied us, and he already knew a lot about this ghetto. No sooner had the guards at the camp entrance seen the two skulls on the collar patch of the uniform of our panzer troops than they let us pass. But we had

Lenin House in Minsk was used by the Wehrmacht as a supply depot. Belorussia, early November 1941.

nothing to do with the SS. The skulls in the centre of our collar patches were the only thing we had in common with the notorious unit.

We encountered sheer misery in the ghetto. However, we had to be very careful: Sergeant Seifenheld had told us that there were informers in here who only pretended to be Jews. From the entrance to the ghetto we went up a slight incline. Then we strolled along a street until we went into a building in search of usable bed frames. Inside we soon found ourselves in a large room, a kind of hall, in which around a hundred Jews were standing close together. No sooner had we entered than Sergeant Seifenheld whispered to us that we should move away from him a little. We immediately suspected that he must have seen someone he knew. We moved aside as ordered. We saw Seifenheld talking to one of the Jews. When he walked away from the Jew and came back to us he was pale as a sheet and looked deeply depressed. He was worn out and was fighting back tears. After he had composed himself he told us that he had just met his master butcher. They were both Berliners and he had known the man since childhood. He told us about this man's good nature and popularity and that he had always been a genuine, kind and honest person.

The master butcher had come here with a small suitcase. He had been told that he could resettle there. But he expressed his concerns to Seifenheld because everything had seemed so strange to him. The sergeant did not have the heart to tell the doubtful man the truth, because Seifenheld knew that his acquaintance would soon be killed. So he placated him and said that the story about the resettlement would indeed turn out to be right. To meet a friend in this situation and to not be able to help him affected our officer deeply.

After we had found three bed frames in one of the rooms in here we left the building again. A truck with a canvas cover was parked in front of the house, and SS personnel were standing around next to it. Sergeant Seifenheld started talking to them. The SS men boasted about what happened to the transport – the truck was fully loaded with Jews. Every day a street was 'cleared': that was around 3,000 Jews day after day who were loaded up and killed. Small children were first killed in the camp so that they would not scream during the transport. They were grabbed by one leg, thrown against the wall, thrown into the truck, and buried in the woods outside Borisov. Older children and adults first had to dig a ditch there, strip naked and stand at the edge of the ditch. Then they were shot.

The next in line gathered up the pieces of clothing that were lying around and then scooped up the corpses. Then a new trench was created, and they were executed in the same way. This process was called 'restacking'. While the SS people were talking another canvas-covered truck drove up. It stopped right next to us, it was empty. The driver got out and then got into the fully loaded vehicle – both vehicles belonged to the Wehrmacht.

We certainly knew that this was being done to the Jews. But I had neither heard of such a level of mass killing as was taking place here in the woods outside Borisov, nor had I ever witnessed one. I shuddered, and I was glad to be able to leave the camp again.

The Gareis family was very grateful to us for the bed frames that we had brought with us from the ghetto. When our stay came to an end after about two weeks, they said goodbye to us with tears in their eyes. We picked up the vehicles in the workshop and drove back to Bryansk. We agreed to stop in Smolensk and spend the night there. After about 80 kilometres we found ourselves in the middle of a forest in the Borisov region, and one of the wheel nuts on our car came loose. We could not drive any further. The others were already out of sight. So the lieutenant who was in the car with me hitchhiked back to Minsk to get the necessary parts from a spare-parts depot. I stayed back with the car on my own. The area around here was not safe; normally you would have only driven through it in a convoy, and now I was alone there. While I was waiting, a Russian with an armband came by – I did not know the meaning of the armband at the time.

Today, though, I suspect that this man was working for the Germans; he probably also fulfilled some function in the systematic extermination of the Jews that was taking place here near Borisov. At the time, however, I was only thinking about my own safety and would not let him go until the lieutenant was back. I gave him some chocolate and asked in Russian – I knew the odd word – if he wanted a cigarette. I tried to stall him, but when he finally wanted to leave I made it unmistakably clear to him by reaching for my pistol that he should preferably stay. I treated him kindly, but now he was my prisoner. After more than two hours the lieutenant came back and we were able to repair the damage. We kept the Russian there until the car was cranked and we could drive on relieved at full throttle. We stayed overnight in Smolensk as agreed. Our lieutenant met a nice Russian girl there, and the two of them got along very well straight away. They talked openly about the current political situation and I heard her say that we were going to lose the war. The lieutenant did not counter this; perhaps he suspected that she was right.

The next day we drove on. We soon saw more and more corpses lying around by the side of the road. We were puzzled: had these people been victims of partisans? We were not at all comfortable with it. After a while we caught up with a transport of several hundred Russian prisoners who were only guarded by two soldiers. Many a prisoner therefore believed that he could easily escape, but that was a fatal mistake. Every fugitive was mercilessly gunned down. We followed the convoy for a while, and when one of the two prison guards said no to our lieutenant's question if we should send reinforcements, we drove on to Bryansk. When we arrived, my unit was no longer there. It had already set off to join the attack on Moscow.

Chapter Ten

War knows no mercy

Even without my unit having received new anti-tank assault guns, it had been integrated into Colonel General Guderian's panzer group. I had no choice but to catch up with my unit. So I set out for Moscow with the entourage of stragglers who mainly transported supplies. We moved on by foot or by horse and sledge, reading from the signs at the forks in the roads which direction the units were heading. The first snow had already fallen around 10 October, and in November the thermometer dropped to minus 50 degrees within a few days. Now we had another enemy besides the Russians, known as 'General Winter'. We only had summer clothing with us, and everyone had to look out for how they could get something warm. I took the pants and fur cap from a dead Russian. Bit by bit I got hold of even more items of clothing in this way, and in the end I was wearing a total of five pairs of trousers on my body to protect me from the freezing cold.

The Russians were superior to us in this respect: they had sufficient winter equipment and had also counterattacked. The situation had changed. Hitler's delusion that he would have defeated the Russians by the onset of winter had senselessly cost innumerable lives.

No sooner had I caught up with my unit at the end of November than we had to retreat. We were in the Tula area, about 200 kilometres from Moscow. We had suffered great losses in soldiers and vehicles. The mood was bad. It was only when it was announced that we would be getting new assault guns that a little hope began to grow. The seven new tanks that we were to pick up at a train station – I have forgotten the name of the place – had been standing around in the cold for three days. How were we supposed to start the vehicles at these temperatures? Everything was frozen solid with ice and we could not lose any time. I could forget about cranking it up, that would not work. As a tank mechanic I had to come up with something. I immediately ordered that wood be fetched and that wooden

During the advance towards Moscow the soldiers found a safe in this municipal building, but there were only stamps in it. Russia, November 1941.

huts be demolished for it too. The huts were inhabited, but given our situation we had no other choice. The people who lived in the already wretched buildings became homeless. War knows no mercy. I also had the rubber rollers of the tanks dammed up with snow on both sides. As soon as the wood was there we piled it up under the middle of the vehicle and set it on fire. It took a whole day for us to get the first vehicle going. It was frustrating. By the time the last of the seven tanks was ready to go the Russian troops had almost caught up with us. They were less than a kilometre away. We moved out away from there as quickly as we could. In the transport train that had brought the tanks there were also soldiers who were supposed to continue on to some front or another, but they ended up going nowhere – they were all frozen to death.

During the retreat, as Christmas was slowly approaching, we gathered up dead comrades who had fallen in the struggle against the Russians. We buried them, or rather covered them with snow, in a small town not too far from Maloarchangelsk, that is between Orel and Kursk. I have forgotten the name of the place. We spent a few days there. Vehicles and sleighs passed the place every day, all of them carrying dead comrades. We unloaded them and improvised a makeshift funeral mass.

The assault guns, which had frozen solid due to the cold, could only be warmed enough to start by lighting fires beneath them. Tula area, late November 1941.

Consecration of the dead by the chaplain. During the retreat from Moscow there was no time for burials. The frozen corpses were stacked up on top of each other and covered with snow. December 1941.

We then drove back to Maloarchangelsk. There we received the order: 'The front will remain here! Live or die here!' This was positional warfare. At this point, however, it was clear that we would lose the war: the whole world was against us, as I as just a 'little man' had also noticed. We had not been in the town long before an SS officer came to our own commanding officer and said that he needed two assault guns.

When he granted him these, there was more: 'Raffeiner, you are coming with me!' I suspected that the mission would be a tough one. I had already seen twice how we had had to get the SS out of a tricky situation. I had my experiences of them and regarded the SS men as reckless, often head-long types. Our commanding officer probably knew that too, because he warned us to turn back if the situation was hopeless. Our group, which consisted of two tanks and nine people, including the SS officer, had to keep our eyes and ears open and use our own brains. Blind bravado was not our thing. We set out, and after about 20 kilometres we came to a small farmhouse. The SS man was very reticent, and we did not know what to expect. Even our lieutenant did not know what was going on; he was in the same tank as me. At a small kolkhoz thirty SS men camouflaged in white clothing were waiting for us. They had organized the same number of horse-drawn sleighs, so-called *panje* sleighs. In the evening we learned from the soldiers that their SS unit had been surrounded by the Russians and that we were to get them out. It was a unit of the SS division *Großdeutschland*, or so the name strips on the sleeves had made me believe at the time. However, as I recently learned, this division had these special strips on its sleeves just like the SS, but *Großdeutschland* was actually an infantry division of the Wehrmacht and was also involved in numerous war crimes. At that time as I say, however, I was convinced that we were dealing with the SS.

It kicked off at dawn, at an icy minus 50 degrees: the tank in front, the thirty sleighs with provisions, weapons and ammunition in the middle, and the second tank following. After about 20 kilometres we came to a small plateau. Below to our right we saw the town of Russkii Brod, above to our left we saw Russian outposts. We also observed that the SS had become involved in a firefight down in the town. We fired our artillery down at Russkii Brod a couple of times to support them.

Further on our journey we believed that we had spotted Russians lying in position directly in front of us. I was supposed to get my submachine gun ready, but it was unusable because it was frozen up. The sleighs fanned out, we were about 300 metres away. No shot had yet been fired. We were relieved to find that we had mistaken deeply snowed-in anti-tank traps for soldiers lying down.

At the end of the plateau there was a steep embankment with a gradient of about 35 degrees, and down below there was a small village. Despite the steepness we made it safely to the bottom. We had arrived at the strong point, and here the train of the *Großdeutschland* division had gathered. It was 22 December 1941, two days before Christmas Eve. We learned that the unit numbered only 170 men and had only two machine guns. Now things happened in quick succession: in the morning we drove the Russian soldiers out of the first village and supplied our people with provisions, machine guns and ammunition. In the afternoon the same action was repeated in the next village. But the next morning the Russians were there again; they came like ants.

We slowly ran out of supplies, especially fuel. We feared that we would not be able to get back to our own troops at all. On the day before Christmas, our lieutenant said to the officer of the division, who at the time I believed was a member of the SS: 'If you can't get us a barrel of petrol by tomorrow, we're out of here.' And sure enough they managed overnight to get the fuel between the Russian sentries. We took the petrol, but still the situation changed: 'We're getting out of here, the Russians will trap us!' We were faced with the problem of how we were to get the heavy tanks up the steep slope in the snow. First we had to wait for it to get dark. At 2pm it was already beginning to get dark and we could start our departure. The front had already moved about half a kilometre and time was pressing. With great difficulty we got up the first tank. The snow was still hard and luckily the tank did not sink down into it. We pulled the second one up with the help of the first tank with tow ropes and chains. It sank into the snow, but the first tank was able to pull it out. It was by that time 11pm on Christmas Eve. We were ordered to torch the village – the old war tactic of 'scorched earth', as it was called. Everything that could not be held was to be destroyed. 'At home, the sacristan will be lighting up the candles for Christmas mass at this moment, and meanwhile we are lighting up the huts of innocent people with our torches!' This thought crossed my mind, but an order was an order. The people became homeless when it was extremely cold. That was our Christmas. But there was no time for long, sentimental reflections during the war. We had to see to it that we would get out safely ourselves. Had the Russians not been so afraid of our assault guns it would have been easy for them to completely surround us and we would have been goners.

Luckily we got out in one piece, and at around five o'clock in the morning we finally reached a village where we could take a breather. Some had to be transported to the nearest hospital with frostbitten toes. I was spared this because I had walked next to the tank and constantly moved my toes in my shoes. Once again we rumbled into the huts and lay down exhausted on the floor to rest a little. It was not the first time that we set up shop 'unannounced' in the inhabited huts. The Russian women, children and old people in there had to put up with us. What else could they do? Only once did a Russian woman show us with her behaviour that she did not like our intrusion. Again and again she spat on the straw on the clay floor that we wanted to sleep on. An officer in my unit – I do not remember his name anymore – asked her several times to stop. When she continued on anyway he threw her out of the hut. Outside it was down to 50 degrees below zero.

In the wooden huts there were often small, simple wood fireplaces that, depending on the season, were only fired with steppe grass. The stove often did not provide enough heat for our troops. So we stoked it up with everything we could find. Sometimes it happened that we set the whole wooden hut on fire and had to flee from the dwelling. We were no saints – not while advancing and certainly not now while retreating. Especially not when we were hungry and had to fill up our 'food box' with provisions because our own supply was nowhere near enough. Then we had to get 'organized' a bit, as we said at the time. Once we raided a small village and slaughtered hens, ducks and other livestock. We entered the huts, looted the cellars and looked for traces of buried food in the clay floor. What were the villagers going to do? There were only women, children and old people – the men were all off fighting. Naturally they cried when we took their livestock away from them. But I had no feelings of guilt. In this world it was normal, it was not a crime, even if that is not understood in today's world. That was war, that was part of it, it was about survival.

Back to our retreat: it was Christmas Day. Our lieutenant could not calm down: he got into one of the two tanks with a few men and looked for an escape route that would lead us safely back to our unit. He knew things could get tricky. The men of the *Großdeutschland* division would scarper if necessary, we could not rely on them. The lieutenant was gone and never came back either. After a short rest we were woken up at around seven o'clock with the words: 'Alarm, the Russians are coming!' We saw the last of the presumed SS men disappear with their sleighs. There were four of us and we stood there alone with our tank. The highest ranking among us was a sergeant, and he now took command. We got up and drove off. It was indescribably cold, and there was a blizzard sweeping through the area to boot. We saw next to nothing in the snowstorm. Suddenly there was shooting from the forest; we turned around and drove in a different direction, and again the Russians shot at us. We danced around aimlessly like this the whole morning. We were all getting nervous, we were trapped. Just as a Russian plane was about to bomb us the snowstorm became so violent that you could not see a thing any more. We could not go a step further and had to stop. The plane circled overhead. We panicked, yelled at each other, and were convinced that this was the end. After a while the storm cleared and I discovered a church tower ahead of us in the white landscape. I tried to calm the mood and asked the loader, whose name was Ros, if he also did not remember that we had already passed this church tower. He confirmed this. Now I turned to all three. 'Listen, we have to stick together now or we're doomed!' I began. 'We have to drive over to the church and then to the left, I remember exactly.' However, the sergeant did not believe us. The whole thing ended in a shouting match and an indescribable uproar. Suddenly, with pistol at the ready, Ros tore off the sergeant's headphones with the command microphone and shouted: 'We're taking over command now!' We immediately gave the order to the driver, our words tumbling out: 'Over to the church and then left!' He drove off, swivelled to the left at the church and drove on. In the snow we found the tracks our tank had made. Thank God! We had not been mistaken. I had us stop. Then I turned to the sergeant and said: 'Sergeant, let's shake hands and forget what happened!' The sergeant shook our hands and we put our pistols away and drove on. If he had refused to make peace with us he would not have got away alive. What Ros and I had taken upon ourselves was more than just disobeying orders, and this would have had dire consequences. But the officer kept his word. So we eventually got back to our unit unharmed. They had already given up expecting us to return.

Chapter Eleven

End of a friendship

Back in Maloarchangelsk we celebrated a belated Christmas in a Russian hut. The Russian residents of the hut could not take part as they only celebrate Christmas in January. Ros, who always had his accordion with him, played *Silent Night*, and there was also an exchange of presents. Even Christmas post had come for us – I had received a stiletto knife and a lighter as a present. We basically gave ourselves presents: a Berliner had already gone to his hometown in November to get our 'Christmas presents' in good time. We spent an exhilarating hour until it started once again: 'Up, up, the Russians are coming!' Reality had caught up with us. We had to go back into action, the front had to be defended. Hitler's order was: hold your position at all costs. That meant that we should preferably die than give up land that had already been conquered.

Those days were incredibly tough. Aeroplanes came every half an hour and dropped bombs. The notorious 'Stalin organ' was in action against us day and night. The Katyusha, as the Russians called the Stalin organ, was a swivelling, truck-mounted rocket launcher with almost forty rounds that could be fired off in quick succession. Each time the rockets were fired there was a howling sound. Around the clock every half an hour we were exposed to this infernal machine with its explosive power. Added to this was the dreary, bitterly cold winter. All our nerves were shot. We numbed our fears and suffering with alcohol. During this time I drank a whole litre of schnapps every evening to be able to cope better with what I had experienced. When I think of that time, I have to admit: we were no longer human.

Another order from Hitler was that no prisoners were to be taken. Prisoners had to be killed on the spot. In the best-case scenario no ammunition was to be wasted on this. Once during this time I got into a tricky situation like this myself. A technical sergeant said to me: 'Raffeiner come with me!' We were to 'finish off' some Russian prisoners. 'Sergeant, if you

Comrades with a tank in Maloarchangelsk after the withdrawal from Moscow. December 1941.

give me the order, I must go,' was my answer. I emphasized the 'must' and looked him seriously in the eye. He understood and, luckily for me, went to find someone else. If he had insisted, there would have been no backing down for me. Disobeying an order, it was clear, would be punishable by death. Shortly afterwards I saw a Russian hut and the prisoners within it go up in flames. I was profoundly relieved that I had been spared this terrible task.

You could look the other way regarding the acts of violence that you were not involved in yourself. Only when you were personally confronted with it did it 'come alive' in you and you thought about how you should decide what to do.

On New Year's Day 1942 our commanding officer – I have forgotten the lieutenant's name – called everyone over to wish them a happy new year with a glass of schnapps. When he handed the glass to me only half of the contents were left in it because his hands were shaking so much. It was not just the cold that was to blame: he was also scarred by the fear and the strain of war. In the first few days of January typhoid fever broke out in our group. Lice were what triggered this disease. Our group consisted of eight comrades with whom I lived in a cramped hut that would better be described as a cave. The sick were taken away and we had to remain in quarantine for eight days. It really was a horrible feeling when at night, accompanied by the eerie howling of the Stalin organs, bombs fell from enemy aircraft too and we were locked in and left to our fate! During the attacks we huddled together in corners to shelter ourselves, and we tried to protect our heads with our hands. Once I even stuck my head in the stove door: when in danger, people try to protect their heads first. I would have liked to see this image myself.

One of the compulsory pastimes – that we were actually ordered to do – was the removal and killing of our lice. I got the idea to count them while doing this. Although I did not develop typhoid fever myself I still remember the number: 366, as many days as there are in a leap year.

These pests had also given us amusing moments on another occasion in Maloarchangelsk. Franzl Müller, a good friend of mine, was responsible for calibrating the assault guns. That is why we called him the 'God of Guns'. Franzl had captured an optical device from the Russians. We experimented with this and discovered that a backlit lens could project a slide image. Unfortunately we did not have any pictures. But the idea did

Typhoid-fever patients in quarantine in Maloarchangelsk. In early January 1942 Raffeiner spent a week there while the Red Army bombed the town. Maloarchangelsk, March 1942.

not let go of us. What else did we have that we could showcase? Our choice ended up being something that each of us had in abundance.

We looked for two small pieces of glass, made a closed edge around one piece with chewed-up bread, placed our 'display objects' on top, and carefully pressed the second piece of glass onto the bread border. Then we looked at our slide image. It looked really impressive. We then announced that there would be a cultural evening with a slide show that night. We did not reveal what we would show. In the meantime we stretched out a white sheet on the wall in one room and organized boards and boxes as seating. Then evening came. Everyone came except for those on duty, even the officers. When we started up the 'slide projector', everyone got a great surprise. What had triggered the indescribable laughter? Lice that had tormented each of us enough. Our audience saw how the oversized lice crawled back and forth and wriggled around. The soldiers laughed heartily, and were grateful for this cheering up.

After the time in quarantine we immediately had to return to combat. We drove to a village called Maklaki 30 kilometres away. With our two tanks we were to defend three villages: Maklaki, Livny and Droskovo.

Comrades Lothar Gladrow, Franz Müller and Franz Reichelt. Maloarchangelsk, spring 1942.

Luis Raffeiner in the uniform of the assault-gun detachment with a skull on his lapel and with the ribbon of the *Kriegsverdienstordens zweiter Klasse* (Distinguished Service Order Second Class). Photograph taken by a Russian photographer towards the end of the time in the winter line. Maklaki, March 1942.

Maklaki was the middle one of the three and the strong point of the infantry division. From Maloarchangelsk we were provided with supplies and ammunition by horse-drawn sleigh. Almost every other night we received a signal from a flare as a sign to engage, so we knew which village we had to rush to in order to give assistance. We commuted back and forth between the villages all winter long. If the Russians had attacked all three villages at the same time with only just a few men we would have been doomed.

We had to stand guard every night. The rhythm of the cycle was always the same: standing watch for an hour and a half, sleeping for an hour, and an hour and a half on duty again. Until the next morning. We slept all winter in our clothes along with hand grenades and all the trimmings. Sometimes the Russians would come right up to our hut and we would listen behind barred doors. But nothing ever happened.

One time we got the order from the first lieutenant to bring his personal inventory to Maklaki, where we were stationed with our tanks. The village where the officer's belongings were was around 15 kilometres from Maklaki. For the transport we had to take a *panje* sleigh. However, we voiced our concerns as to whether we would arrive before dark, given the time of day and the cold. 'Oh, you can do it!' was the lieutenant's succinct answer. Then there was nothing left for us – there were two of us – but to carry out the assignment. So we packed the things onto the sleigh, hitched a little horse in front of it, and then we drove off. Soon the horse was slowing down and it was getting darker and darker. The cold bothered both the horse and us greatly. We had tied the reins to the sleigh horn, we were getting increasingly more tired, and I could literally hear an organ playing and bells ringing. It is hard to explain: somehow everything became very easy, I found myself in a state of ecstasy. Now we were about 200 metres from the village. Meanwhile the horse stopped every 10 metres. It was pitch black when we arrived in Maklaki. We just staggered into the digs we had here and were completely exhausted. We had narrowly escaped death through hypothermia. The horse, on the other hand, did not survive.

Spring gradually arrived. It was March, the temperatures were getting a little milder, and we were still in Maklaki. There were countless dead Russians lying around, who had fallen victim to the fighting with our infantry. As the snow melted, *panje* sleighs that had been left behind by the

Luis Raffeiner with a Russian peasant family in a village above Maloarchangelsk. March 1942.

fleeing Germans became visible too. We had to dig these out, clear the snow off them, and position them in such as way as to irritate the enemy. The Russians were to be led to believe that the Germans had returned.

Russian reconnaissance planes soon discovered the sleighs. A short time later the Russians came with fighter planes and bombed us. I found myself with my colleague Franzl Müller behind a hut that had only one room and an exit on both sides. We saw the plane coming, watched the bombs fall one after the other, and ran through the hut as the plane flew past us overhead. We threw ourselves into the bomb crater that had just been created on this side. At the same time, on the other side, where we had just been standing, the next bomb landed. The splinters were stuck all over the walls of the hut and swept over our heads. We had a guardian angel once again! While I could hardly believe the fact that I was still intact, I just felt gratitude inside. There were many situations like this where I miraculously got away unscathed. I owned a set of rosary beads that I did not just carry with me as a lucky charm.

At the end of March 1942 we returned to Maloarchangelsk. Just when we got there we met a large crowd in the village square. Three gallows had been set up in the middle of the square. There were three prisoners

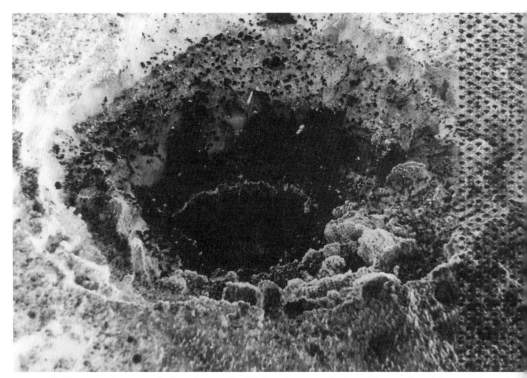

Raffeiner and a comrade found cover in this bomb crater during a Russian bombing attack. Maklaki, March 1942.

standing next to them, who were to be hanged. They were partisans, a woman and two men. Now we also found out the reason for the execution: the whole train, the supply section of my unit, had been stationed here in Maloarchangelsk and had been bombed again and again. Throughout the winter these partisans were believed to have used light signals from the roofs to divulge the position of our unit to the Russian aircraft. The execution was conducted almost like a ceremonial act and served as a deterrent: the people of the town had to watch as the prisoners lynched each other. First, one of the men put the noose around the woman's neck and then knocked the stool away from under her feet. Then the man was hanged by his comrade. The last man was executed by a German soldier. A sign was hung around the neck of each of those hanged on which was written in Russian: 'This is how partisans end up!'

A little while later we were ordered to attack Voronezh, or rather we had to wait for this first. With our battery and an anti-aircraft detachment we were stationed in a small village near Voronezh, close to the river Don. There we waited for further orders and – combat-ready – for Russian units. We were there for three weeks. To stave off boredom each tank crew took turns inviting the other for something to eat. Another time we

A village near Maloarchangelsk. On the ground lies the straw that the partisans used to signal to the Red Army planes where the Russians lived. Spring 1942.

Waiting for the attack on Voronezh. Raffeiner's unit, pictured here whiling away the time, was stationed behind the front for a total of three weeks. Voronezh area, April 1942.

staged a promotion: our lieutenant praised the merits of one or two comrades and 'promoted' them in the presence of all of us. We got a great laugh out of the seriousness with which those chosen accepted their 'honour'. Shortly afterwards, however, we told those 'promoted' the truth. We also arranged a photo session at the request of the female village population. We had learned that the girls wanted to be photographed. So we placed a table with flowers and a bench in front of a cane wall with an entrance and an exit. We threw a white cloth over the seat. The girls could not see what was behind it. Then, after the first two had sat down and were laughing expectantly into the camera, we poured a bucket of water over them. The two were far from happy about it, but when other girls were then 'baptised' by us they too had a laugh about it. So we spent a lovely afternoon where both sides had a right good laugh. We liked to have fun, but never once did any of our tank personnel assault a girl. Our superiors had also warned us about the Russian girls: not only would we catch diseases, they emphasized. The Russian women would castrate us too. That stuck with us.

Russian girls looking forward to being photographed, but a bucket of water hidden above them awaits.

Raffeiner and a peasant woman sitting in front of a shelter and listening to the radio.

Russian peasants marvel at the radio. Raffeiner remembered that *Schwarzsender* (forbidden broadcasts) were occasionally listened to.

Raffeiner mends his comrade's trousers. In the jumping-off position before Voronezh all tanks were camouflaged with straw (background).

Corporal Raffeiner during an exercise. Voronezh area, April 1942.

Afterwards – the summer of 1942 was already approaching – I drove homeward bound. Annual leave was waiting, which I had truly earned. I came to the train station in Ponyri via the forward directing centre at Kursk. From there I went on to South Tyrol by train. Annual leave lasted around three weeks, but with the trips there and back I was away from my unit for much longer. The return trip took longer of course. My parents had opted to emigrate, but they had not yet left.

I had a walk home of one and a half hours from the train station at the entrance to the Schnalstal. On the way I stopped at the inn in Neuratheis. I had a pleasant encounter here when I saw my best friend Bernhard Grüner. We were both delighted to see each other again and the reception was warm. When we left the inn a little later he asked me with obvious interest about the situation with the war in Russia. He was a fanatical Nazi and a functionary with the VKS, the *Völkischer Kampfring Südtirols*. As a functionary Bernhard did not need to go to war. He listened to my stories with a keen interest. I knew he expected only positive things from me, so first I told him about the perfect organization and that there were even film nights and Christmas presents. As we had never kept secrets from each other I also spoke openly of my conviction that we would lose the war. After I said that, he snapped at me. Where would we end up, he barked, if everyone thought that way: after all, this was about our future and that of our descendants. He railed at me and gave me an emotionally charged lecture on Nazi ideology for the rest of the way. A sudden cold took the place of the warm joy of seeing each other again, and I felt hatred flaring up in his words. It was as if I had deeply insulted him personally. I simply replied that we would talk about it again if I survived the war.

When we arrived in the village he left me and did not say another word to me during my entire leave. His attitude could have been very dangerous for me. A soldier with a mind-set like the one I expressed would have a demoralizing effect on the others, which would amount to treason. Such a thing would certainly be punishable by death, I thought. I feared that Bernhard's fanaticism was stronger than our friendship and that he might

On home leave in Karthaus. Luis Raffeiner in his assault-gun uniform, his father Josef, his mother Aloisia, and sister Maria. July 1942.

Raffeiner shows his friend Karl Gurschler (commonly known as 'Tanzhaus Karl', and a former comrade in the Italian Army) his Distinguished Service Cross Second Class. *Tanzhaus* Inn in Unser Frau, Schnals, July 1942.

report me to my unit. I was very worried and broke off my leave two days early to talk to Bernhard's father, who had emigrated to Lienz in East Tyrol, about the incident with Bernhard. I urged him to write his son a letter and to put in a good word for me. Bernhard's father was a sensible man who liked me and took my concerns seriously. He promised to write to Bernhard.

I passed the following days and weeks with excruciating uncertainty. The intervention of Bernhard's father had the desired effect, I was off the hook, but it was a personal lesson for me. Fanaticism can destroy the very best friendship!

Chapter Twelve

Attack on Stalingrad

Before I reported back from leave I visited a friend in Ottnang in Upper Austria, who had sent me post and some parcels. Her name was Frieda and she and my sister had trained together as midwives. Before my holiday she had sent me a card saying that she had been transferred from Berlin to Ottnang. For this reason I arrived a day late to the registration office in Kobel near Rosenheim. I tried to blame my delay on an air raid, but I could not get away with my little lie because they would have known about it here. I was referred to another official who I got along better with. I pulled out a bottle of wine and a couple of cigarettes, and my papers were then back in order and the matter was settled. My journey led me back to Russia, initially to the forward directing centre at Kursk. There I found out that my unit had already moved on and was no longer subordinated to Army Group Centre, but to another Army Group. I now had to go south towards the Don. On the road of advance there was a whole forest of signs at every junction. Each unit provided information about its direction of advance, everything was perfectly organized. There was no shortage of lifts either, the road was very busy in both directions. It was the end of July 1942 and I crossed the Don near Zimlyansk. I drove on via Bataisk and Salsk to the Kalmyk Steppe, which lay north-west of the Caspian Sea.

I was travelling in a truck with two comrades whom I did not know. We drove down the taxiway. Before dark we looked for a place to stay in a field and dug a pit for this. Then we parked the vehicle camouflaged with grass and sunflowers directly over the pit for our protection. We had a quiet night, but at dawn we were awakened by strange noises. My pulse quickened, someone was outside! 'The Russians!' was my first thought. We took the rifles, and with our finger on the trigger we crouched tensely in our hide-out. We could not identify the noises. We waited anxiously in our pit, but nothing happened. Neither friend nor foe made themselves known. We crawled cautiously from our overnight camp and saw legs in front of us. It was camel legs. Two camels were standing in front of us, chewing the sunflowers we had used for camouflage! Our tension turned to roaring laughter. We were in the Kalmyk Steppe: there were camels here, which were also used for combat purposes, especially for the transport of weapons and supplies. The beasts were practical and frugal, but they could only be used to a limited extent. The animals could not be let go as far as the front, otherwise they would alert the enemy with their wailing. Before they came within tell-tale earshot the transport would be halted and the supplies taken further another way.

For me, the journey continued on towards Astrakhan, a city on the Volga north of the Caspian Sea. It took sixteen days to reach my unit somewhere near Astrakhan. It was now August 1942 and we were preparing for the attack on Stalingrad. A little while later it began. At the end of August we reached the Volga, on which Stalingrad lies, at Krasnomarskoe.[8] The fighting for the city had already started. We fired with our tanks at the factories on the islands on the Volga, the islands in the river from which the Russians shot at us. Occasionally they also called over to

Luis Raffeiner on a camel in the Kalmyk Steppe. August 1942.

In the Kalmyk Steppe before Stalingrad. The unit had to wait more than a week for a tank to be repaired. Raffeiner is seen here eating his first melon. September 1942.

us: 'Comrades, come over to us, bring your mess kit and coat!' And: 'Now let's make a little marching music!' The invitation boomed loudly and eerily through the microphone. They then fired their artillery pieces, and we now felt very differently because of the way things were whistling around us.

Bullets and bombs rained down on us like mad, it was chaotic. We were rushed back and forth with our tanks, we were needed as reinforcements everywhere. It was almost impossible to keep track of where you were in this situation. At the beginning of October a large part of Stalingrad was reduced to ashes. Factories and houses were razed to the ground, the burst clouds were leaden in the air and obscured the sun. The 6th Army under General Friedrich Paulus had surrounded the city and Hitler had ordered it to be starved into submission.[9]

Our assault-gun unit was also indirectly subordinated to Paulus. It was November 1942 and there was already snow on the ground. We were ordered to collect new tanks at the railway station at Kamenka 80 kilometres from Stalingrad. There was a break in the fighting at this time, only a few shots could be heard. As it later turned out, it was the calm before the storm. A total of thirty-five men from our unit, including a lieutenant, were supposed to go to Kamenka. My comrade, Sergeant Franz Reichelt, was also part of the group. Franz was a Sudeten German and truly a great guy, my 'partner in crime'. There were only the two of us travelling with the vehicle from the workshop, and it seemed to me that we had the opportunity to have a really nice day after our recent exertions. Specifically, I wanted to snatch a chicken somewhere and fry it. I tried hard to persuade Franz not to follow the rest of the troop until the following day. But he was stubborn and insisted that we should go with the others.

So we drove to Kamenka, where the tanks were ready. They were re-fuelled, calibrated and stocked with ammunition, then we drove to our quarters. It was relaxing not to be in the middle of the hail of bombs and to be able to rest a little. But this cosiness did not last long. Around midnight we heard sledges go by: it turned out to be Hungarians. We thought nothing of it and tried to go back to sleep. At five in the morning there was an alarm: the Russians had broken through. They had freed themselves from our iron ring around Stalingrad! We immediately jumped up onto our tanks and drove towards the front to Stalingrad. After about 30 kilometres we reached a railway station, behind which was an open field. The field was littered with Russian T-34 tanks, it was covered in them. The sight of this model of tank frightened the life out of every German soldier. The colossal threat rolled toward us from about 20 metres away. The lieutenant, a brave guy, gave the order to shoot. We fired shells from behind the protection of the station building and actually managed to stop the horde of tanks for the time being. It was a David versus Goliath struggle: our seven tanks against a whole horde. Our advantage was that the Russians did not know if a second front had built up behind the buildings, so they were careful.

As we later learned, the Russians had launched a counter-offensive and surrounded the German troops in Stalingrad. Of my tank unit, out of a total of 500 soldiers only 35 men were outside the ring, the rest were encircled. We were incredibly lucky! If Franz Reichelt had not insisted the day before that we should go out with the others, we too would have ended up in this hopeless situation. I may be repeating myself – but once again I had the feeling that a higher force had protected me.

We were in retreat: during the day we fought valiantly against the overwhelming Russian forces and tried to hold our position. At night we

Raffeiner with his comrade Franz Biribauer from Hall in Tirol in front of the *Villa Frieda* tent. The wooden shack over the tent protected against the cold at night. September 1942.

Raffeiner picking up new tanks at the Kamenka railway station, 80 kilometres from Stalingrad. November 1942.

Christmas Eve 1942. Raffeiner (with tie) and comrades at their Christmas party during the retreat from Stalingrad.

retreated under cover of darkness. In the meantime Christmas had arrived. On Christmas Eve I put on my tie that I had brought with me for special occasions, because despite the almost hopeless situation we insisted on organizing a Christmas party, even if only for a brief moment. We even had a Christmas tree that we decorated with paper, and a few biscuits.

The situation for us became increasingly more precarious: the infantry supply service, which was supported by our seven tanks, was of little help. Everyone by now was trying to get away as quickly as possible. As our squad only consisted of around thirty men I had to drive the oil truck. The starter was broken and we had no time whatsoever to repair the damage. You could still drive it, but it took two people to start the vehicle. One had to crank the front, while the other stepped on the accelerator. Everyone had scarpered, and suddenly I was alone there. How was I supposed to start the truck now? My pulse rose, the Russians were getting closer. I had to sort out the vehicle somehow. I quickly took the crank, stuck it on the front, and turned it. It jumped back and hit my right arm with enormous force. It was broken. Now the mess was well and truly complete. All my comrades were gone, I had a broken arm, the truck would not start, and the enemy was almost in front of my nose. I first took a long swig of

From 19 January to the end of March 1943 Raffeiner was in the military hospital at Mauer-Öhling near Amstetten (Lower Austria). He is pictured here at the railway station following his release in late March 1943.

His friend Frieda Schander visited Raffeiner in Mauer-Öhling.

schnapps from my canteen. Suddenly I heard a voice: 'Let's go, Raffeiner, jump in, the Russians are after us!' It was a sergeant who came along at the last minute.

'I broke my arm,' I yelled at him. 'Get in and hit the accelerator, I'll crank,' ordered the sergeant. The truck started and we got out of there at the very last moment.

After two days I was taken to the collection point for the wounded, and by this time my arm was completely blue. Relieved, I got on the train in Politoskaya,[10] which first took me to Lublin in Poland. I had already got a makeshift cast. After my stay in Lublin I was taken to the military hospital in Mauer-Öhling in Lower Austria. My arm hurt, to be sure, but I was glad that I was no longer in the middle of the turmoil of war and that I could rest on the trip. When I arrived in Mauer-Öhling on 19 January 1943 and my cast was removed, I felt so relieved. The doctors shook their heads in disbelief: lice had made a veritable road network on the inside of my plaster cast. Those bastards had been torturing me the whole time!

Chapter Thirteen

Calm before the storm

After my recovery I arrived on 28 March 1943 at the barracks of *Sturm-geschützersatzabteilung* 200, my new unit, in Schweinfurt am Main. There I met some comrades who had also been wounded in Russia. Now began a really nice time for me. I found work in the workshop there and put together a bicycle for myself. The bike gave me a bit of freedom, I almost felt like a king. At the weekend I went on excursions with it and explored the area. I was always on the lookout to see if I could find something to eat. There were ration cards, to be sure, but never much food. I often stayed on a farm because that's where people were most likely to have something left over. Soldiers were well respected by the population, and I was warmly welcomed everywhere I went. Until 17 August 1943.

That day I had been assigned to the so-called 'fire watch' with two other comrades. That meant we were to be on the lookout for incendiary bombs dropped by planes. We were on a three-story barracks building in the front part of the barracks area, which was about 3 square kilometres. I was the longest serving of the three of us and was therefore in command. Suddenly we heard planes coming. We had never seen anything like it. Plane after plane, the sky was full of machines. A gigantic American squadron flew overhead and bombed the train station and the nearby *Fichtel und Sachs* ball-bearing factory. The devastation almost took your breath away. Nevertheless we gasped because both the barracks and ourselves had been spared. Shortly afterwards we heard that ominous hum in the air again. A second wave came and began to bomb the barracks. It looked like a dark carpet was floating towards us. At the same time the crackling of the anti-aircraft guns started again, the flak was fired off. When the first bombs fell at the back of the barracks I immediately shouted: 'Get down!' The crashing sound was incessant, and we tumbled down the stairs. At that moment we were struck with a direct hit. We were

Raffeiner and an NCO (a comrade from the Russian campaign) in the workshop of the Schweinfurt am Main tank barracks. On the left is the Sachs light motorcycle that Raffeiner put together himself. Spring 1943.

literally shot down the stairs. The man in front was wounded, the comrade behind me was dead. I miraculously escaped unharmed.

The grounds of the barracks had been devastated by the bombing, and it was a terrible sight. In the garage of a barrack building we found a car that we just managed to get working. We cleared the debris away and drove out into the country to a nearby village, where we spent the night. In Schweinfurt the US Army squadron had also dropped phosphorus bombs that night, i.e. incendiary bombs. Many residents, so we were told, ran into the street like burning torches and screamed horribly. After the attack it said in the newspaper that around a thousand aircraft had bombed Schweinfurt in two waves, that would have been 500 per squadron. However, this information was not true: it was later found out to have been far fewer.

After the attack on Schweinfurt it was said that the assault-gun detachment would go to Dalherda in the Rhön Mountains in central Germany.

Since this mountain village in Hesse is about 700 metres above sea level and the way up was steeper than average, it had to be clarified beforehand if the supply system would function properly. So we first inspected the flat area in question, which covered around 40 square kilometres. Dalherda was an evacuated village exclusively used by the military and could be reached in an hour's walk from Schmalnau below. After we had assured the officers that supplies would also get to us in winter, we settled in up here. We set up a training camp for radio courses, the *Wildflecken* military training ground, and lived here in a very civilized manner in a proper house. My main task was the maintenance and repair of the six wood-gas trucks. These vehicles were powered by wood gas: a stove in the vehicle was fired with square wooden blocks that were carried on the flatbed. Maintaining these trucks was quite a dirty job.

Although we were in the middle of the war, we spent a quiet, almost peaceful time here. I always had Saturday and Sunday off, and there was 94 hours of holidays for me to use up. I often drove to Innsbruck. Once I also went home to get my skiing gear. When the lieutenant saw my ski poles on my return he wanted me to sell them to him. That was out of the question, but I promised I could get him some. 'Good,' he said, 'I hope you're going on a break again soon!'

Luis Raffeiner with his brother Peter. The photograph was taken during home leave in Meran while he was stationed in Dalherda, 1943.

Then I made my written request for leave, which read: 'I request the company for leave, my mother is seriously ill.' When I showed the lieutenant the request, he smiled and said: 'Don't forget me then!'

My leave was approved and the pass was issued at the guardhouse. I was about to put both it and the return ticket in my pocket when the NCO changed his mind and told me to pick up the papers the next morning. The next day I was already in holiday mood. I did not want to walk for an hour down to the railway station, so I asked a colleague to take me there in the boss's car. Once there, he wished me a nice holiday and drove back. I was studying the train timetable when it suddenly occurred to me that I had forgotten my leave pass and tickets. I immediately ran into the station building and asked for an urgent call to the Dalherda training ground. This way I let my colleague know to bring my papers down with the motorcycle as quickly as possible, because the train would be leaving in about fifteen minutes. At the last second my colleague rushed up and handed the papers to me. I just managed to climb up into the last carriage as the train was already pulling away.

After my break I returned with a pair of beautiful new ski poles that I had bought in a shop in Meran. I was immediately called into the office. 'Oh, no,' I thought to myself, 'all hell is going to break loose!' The audacity I had shown when starting my leave would not go unpunished. In the office I was told: 'Go into the boss immediately!' I went in with ski poles in hand, put them down at his desk and stood in front of him with a stern posture and the snappy greeting 'Raffeiner reporting back from leave!' The lieutenant looked at me and said with a smile: 'Well, Raffeiner, I've never seen a holidaymaker like you: first you use my car without permission, then forget the leave pass, and then order a motorcyclist from the training ground to bring you your pass!' He wanted to show me that he knew about everything. I justified myself by saying that otherwise I would not have been able to get him the ski poles. He laughed and said 'fine' and handed me 20 marks. I did not want to take the money, but he insisted and said I should get myself a beer with it.

Soon afterwards the first sergeant came up to me. He was someone who liked to look out for people and asked me if I could get him a padlock for his canteen because his schnapps was always being stolen. At that time there was almost nothing left to be had, because while we lived an almost leisurely life here, the cities throughout Germany were constantly being bombed. A week later I was already on leave in South Tyrol again and returned with a new padlock. The sergeant thanked me and that evening bought me a schnapps. In general there was almost a comradely and friendly atmosphere in the camp between the ordinary soldiers and the officers. That would change soon.

So the year 1943 passed, and in January 1944 our unit was transferred to Schieratz/Sieradz in Poland, around 50 kilometres southwest of Łódź. The mood shifted, and it was all business again. Here I made use of my annual leave. When I came back from my holiday I learned that I was the only one from *Sturmgeschützabteilung* 200 who was to be transferred to Borna near Leipzig. A new training department was set up there and I was to be assigned as a tank maintenance instructor. Before I left for Borna my comrade and friend Willi Heinze from Hirschberg asked me a favour. Willi was the lieutenant's right-hand man and had access to my pay book, which, in addition to my personal data, had all holidays recorded in it: on a single sheet of paper the annual leave that had also just been taken. Willi wanted to take this sheet out and stick in a new, blank sheet of paper so I could get another annual leave in Borna as they would not find one in the pay book there any more. I was not entirely comfortable with it, but Willi did it perfectly. He even put the necessary stamp on the new sheet. That was his parting present for me.

When I arrived in Borna in July 1944 I was immediately asked: 'Raffeiner, when was the last time you were on leave?' 'A year and a half ago' was my answer. 'I was just indispensable, and now I've been transferred here to Borna.' I felt a bit queasy, but I had to go through it. A look at the booklet confirmed my statement. 'You're going on leave immediately' came the command back. 'Go to the clothing store, hand in your things there, and you'll be gone by one o'clock!' 'Yes, Lieutenant,' I shouted back, and soon afterwards I was on my way to Innsbruck to the registration office for all South Tyrolers. The old sergeant at the desk who drew up the papers for the journey across the border knew me from my previous holidays. When he saw me, he was puzzled and asked: 'Are you only coming now? You should have come eight days ago because your father has died. We sent a telegram to Schieratz!'

In Schieratz I had not been told anything about the passing of my 83-year-old father, and nothing had been known about it in my new unit. So I drove home with subdued joy, but was still happy that I was allowed to go back home and could be there for my mother for a while. After father's death my sister Maria, who had not emigrated, stayed with our mother in a small apartment in the post office building in Karthaus. At the end of this holiday I left my camera that I had recorded my previous war experiences with at home. I had a vague feeling that harder times were coming my way.

Chapter Fourteen

'Run, Raffeiner, the war is over'

After my home visit I drove back to Borna in the autumn of 1944 with mixed feelings. I was to start my service as a tank maintenance instructor here. But this never happened in the end. As soon as I arrived I had to pack my things and take the train on to the Eastern Front. Alone and among a lot of strange comrades, I drove to Skarżysko-Kamienna, about 150 kilometres southeast of Łódź. I was to report to the forward directing centre. Once I got to the Polish city, the way to the forward directing centre turned out to be considerably dangerous. First I heard a hum in the air, then the plane was already above me. Immediately afterwards it fired down at us, I threw myself on the ground and rolled to the side. The plane made a turn, came back, and the rattling started again. This happened a few times, and half rolling and half running I finally reached the forward directing centre, where I reported for the assault-gun detachment of the tank destroyers. As luck would have it the lieutenant of my new unit was there too, so I was able to travel with him.

No one said a word along the way. It was already dark when we reached the unit via a circuitous route. I was registered as a newcomer. I did not even have time to look around for a moment. I had to go straight to the front line, down into the trenches, where the enemy bullets whistled around my ears to the left and right as a greeting. How I felt at that moment is difficult to describe. For months I had lived without seeing combat and travelled home frequently. Suddenly I was sent to a completely new unit to be literally thrown into the trenches, surrounded by complete strangers. There was no time for me to get my bearings, everything was strange. My morale was at zero, and the thought occurred to me: 'Now the final hour has struck.'

After a while someone came and finally got me out of this situation. Fortunately I had to relieve a tank driver who was allowed to watch a film in the camp further back. It was all so unbelievable: to the front the war in which people were killing each other was raging – and a little further back films were being shown. But for me it was salvation: I would have been a dead man in the trenches if I had stayed any longer.

In September 1944 the Russians gradually pushed us further and further back. We spent the winter near the Dukla Pass on the Polish-Slovakian border, and we celebrated the New Year at the village innkeeper's in Nižná Polianka, a few kilometres beyond the Slovakian border. The inn was a room with a clay floor, like in a goat stable. There was plenty of schnapps flowing, we laughed and joked, nothing mattered now anyway, you could be dead tomorrow. The landlord was a nice chap, and when we left he cried. We were pushed back further and further by the Russians. We went via Mährisch-Ostrau/Ostrava in the present-day Czech Republic towards Upper Silesia. We reached the village of Jabłonka not far from the Polish border through a mountain pass. Here we stayed in the *Auschwitz* café. The owner of the café was a dyed-in-the-wool Nazi, but he had already been frightened off and had allegedly fled to Austria, to Styria. We stayed in his elegant house and rummaged around in it to our hearts' content. In the attic I found a saucepan and a lid with a bird on it. It was a kind of pressure cooker. Now we wanted to know what the bird was for, whose wings could even move. We went into the kitchen, put the pot with water and lid on the heated stove and waited eagerly to see what would happen. When the water boiled in the pot, the bird began to chirp, flap its wings, and wiggle its rear end. All the soldiers standing around the stove burst out laughing. It was just nice to laugh again. It was liberating.

There was also a hardware shop in the town, whose owner had also fled. That was of course an interesting treasure trove: I pulled up the shop's shutters and immediately started looking for a storm lantern that worked with kerosene. There were another dozen soldiers in the shop with me rummaging around. Soon the contents of all the drawers were emptied out onto the floor, and the things were lying around half a metre high in the shop. After I had found a lantern I went upstairs with a colleague to the bedroom and discovered an alarm clock on the bedside table that I could also put to good use. We used the bedroom with its beautiful parquet floor and pull-out beds as lodgings for the night. Sleeping in these beds was very comfortable, and we were incredibly happy to have this luxury.

Up to that point it had been rather quiet in Jabłonka; only a few shots could be heard every now and then. But one morning all hell broke loose here too. There was a terrible barrage. The Russians were advancing inexorably, and we were again forced to flee as quickly as possible. It was the spring of 1945, and we reached Olmütz/Olomouc. We stayed here for the time being and held our position.

It was early morning on 9 May 1945. We were in Mährisch-Sternberg/ Šternberk, north of Olmütz, and we were engaged in fighting. Our situation was miserable. We had almost run out of petrol. In order to save the little fuel we had left for our remaining vehicles we took unusual measures. We dismantled railway tracks and used them as connectors between the vehicles. The front one, a tracked vehicle, served as a kind of tractor, with the remaining vehicles being pulled along. Apart from petrol we also lacked spare parts for our vehicles. That day we were in an old Ford made in Cologne heading towards our position when I discovered a burned-out car of the same model below the road. I could do with some parts from the car, especially since the wheel bolts on the back of our car were completely worn out. So no sooner had I got to our position than I quickly put on my blue overalls, got into the maintenance truck, and drove about a kilometre back to the abandoned vehicle.

I was busy dismantling the brake drum when a tank from our unit drove past me. Someone shouted something incomprehensible at me. I did not think anything about it at that time. Then the next tank came along. That struck me as strange, though. Everyone knew that things were not going well for us, but I could not believe that we were capitulating. The day before, our boss had given a fiery speech that was followed by unbelievably jubilant enthusiasm. Among other things, he had said: 'Well, comrades, if Admiral [the original has General here but he was in fact a Grand Admiral] Dönitz is allowed to free up the Western Front, then we will defeat Bolshevism, the Russian colossus, with the German Wehrmacht!' Such were the visions we were confronted with. The bogeyman that was portrayed to us was always the communist peril. At the time, however, we did not know that Hitler was dead, nor that the previous commander-in-chief of the Navy, Karl Dönitz, had taken his place as Reich President and was trying to secure a partial peace with the Western Allies in order to repel the advancing Red Army in Germany.

So that day I could not quite believe that the tanks that were passing by were actually fleeing. But when the third tank came by and a comrade shouted, 'Run, Raffeiner, the war is over', there was no longer any doubt.

Now I felt different. I ran around the corner where my vehicle was parked and wanted to get in quickly. It was burning. One of our people had already set it on fire. During the retreat everything was always destroyed: every house, every vehicle, everything. Now I was literally alone there with nothing left. The last tank had driven past even though they had seen me. So I had no choice but to run. After about 3 kilometres I finally caught up with my comrades, but we could go no further. Russian anti-tank obstacles were blocking the way. In this turmoil a car suddenly drove up. Some officer got out, fetched a box from the car and handed out the service record books that were in it to the soldiers who had rushed past. So I got my own one back. In addition to my rank – I had been promoted to *Stabsgefreiter* (staff lance corporal) – it also had my personal data plus a photo and the various locations where we had served. But I did not keep it for long: when I went into captivity I burned it.

The war was over; now everyone had to contemplate how to get away from it all. In the meantime it was total chaos. Thousands upon thousands of soldiers were fleeing. I teamed up with my sergeant. We found a jeep, got in, and were happy to be able to drive as far as the fuel would take us. We found ourselves in an indescribable cloud of dust. Everyone was trying to scramble away, and as quickly as possible: some with a vehicle they had snatched, others on horseback, sometimes with carts or sometimes running. Everything was in motion. Anything that was no longer of any use or that was a hindrance was left behind or thrown away. Dead Czechs were lying around. They had set up an anti-tank obstacle to stop the flood of refugees, but they could not. Our aim was to get to the Americans, as we did not want to end up in Russian captivity under any circumstances.

At dawn we drove through a small town, where the street reminded me of the pergolas in Meran: narrow and flanked by houses on both sides. The Russians had bombed the town that night to make it difficult for the Germans to escape. They naturally wanted to take prisoners. If the Russians paid us back for what we had done to them, then God help us, I thought. Houses were burning on both sides of the street. Burning beams tumbled down: the sergeant was driving, he hit the accelerator, and we raced through with our heads ducked down. We were incredibly lucky and made it through unscathed.

The next obstacle was a hill with a steep downward slope. The valley floor below was enveloped in a gigantic cloud of dust, kicked up by the countless refugees and clouded over by plumes of smoke from the burning vehicles. We waited until the visibility improved, then the sergeant drove us straight down the steep 500-metre slope. The journey with the jeep soon ended because we ran out of petrol. Now we continued on foot. Unfortunately we did not have the same options as our Field Marshal, Ferdinand Schörner. He had always been a much feared general, but once the war was lost he acted like a cowardly dog. He escaped dressed in Bavarian costume by plane and left the soldiers of his Army Group to their fate. Ever since this episode he has now only been known as 'Bavarian Seppl'.

We, on the other hand, were greeted on a hill by a Russian tank. An officer told us to throw down our weapons, we could all go home. Naturally we wanted to go home, so we did what we were told. But our escape seemed to be slowly leading to a dead end. More and more we saw armed Czech police officers in civilian clothes flanking the stream of refugees. Soon they were standing at intervals of 30 or 40 metres on either side. It was about 300 kilometres from Olmütz to the line where the Americans were. We were hoping to be able to get there. But now that was wishful thinking. The sergeant and I parted: we saw this as the only hope of getting through to the Americans.

At first I tried to get hold of some provisions. I found a small empty rucksack, then rummaged around in an abandoned car. There I found a loaf of bread, a box of cheese spread and a little bag of poppy seeds. That was my marching provisions. At the next crossroads I stopped and wondered anxiously which way might lead me to freedom. I can no longer say whether I ultimately chose to go left or right. I only know that shortly afterwards I came upon a Czech sentry post. There was a cornfield beside the road, and further back a house. When the guard asked me where I was going, I replied that I wanted to drink water from the well in the field. Thinking that I had cleverly got away with it, I ran into the next guard at the well. I was getting water from the well when someone came out of the nearby house. A man in a white coat came up to me. He was very un-friendly when I wanted to ask him about the current situation in the area.

But when he found out that I was Austrian his temperament changed and he even asked me into the house for coffee. I asked him again about the current situation because we had received no information at all at the front. He told me that the Russians were at the rivers Oder and Neisse, that Berlin had been taken, and that Bavaria had become a *Freistaat* (Free State) again. He also said that the Germans were being brought to the nearby airport in Deutschbrod/Havlíčkův Brod and that there was no chance of getting through because the Czechs had sealed everything off. Then he gave me one of the horses that was running around and suggested it would be best if I turned myself in to the Russians at the airport. I took the horse, but soon let it go, and then presented myself to the Russians. The first thing they did was to take the few things I was carrying with me. But they did not get my watch, which I had carefully sewn under the lining of my cap. This precaution would later save my life.

Chapter Fifteen

'The dead can't harm us'

I was one of around 170,000 men who were trapped here in Deutschbrod. Organized distribution of provisions was out of the question in view of such an enormous number of people. If I had known what was in store for me I would not have left the little bag of bran lying there so carelessly that I had found in a coach on a trip around the airport. Later I thought about it with much regret.

The rumour soon went around that the Austrians would be released. We even formed our own committee, and it was arranged that we should gather in groups of a hundred men each. The swastika flags were taken out of the aircraft that were lying around: red, white and red flags were made out of them, attached to a stick, and every hundred people now received an Austrian flag. Altogether there was a total of 1,800 Austrians in the prison camp. The groups of one hundred were divided into three companies. Each company presented the Russians with a list of names with their place of origin and information on where each of the soldiers intended to go. We did not have to wait long. The Russians gave my company, 500 men, permission to march. In Iglau/Jihlava we spent a whole day on a slope in the blazing sun. I carefully divided my bread into small rations because there were no provisions. Next we arrived in Brünn/Brno.

It was already the end of May when I was sitting in a shell crater with my comrade Hans Bachlechner from Defereggental in East Tyrol and we were pondering how we could get something to eat. He sat there crying because his loaf of bread, his only piece of food, had been stolen from him overnight. I gave him some of my meagre stash, and we agreed that we would share everything and help each other in other ways. Suddenly my gaze fell on a building that looked like a hospital. I knew that there were kitchenettes there where I could find something to eat. A Russian guard was on duty in front of the building – but at the right moment I sneaked in. The hospital was empty, and I found nothing in the kitchenette except a few tea bags. Now I had to hurry back to my company, otherwise they would have marched on without me. Suddenly I got the unmistakable smell of germinating potatoes. It was coming up from the cellar shaft that I had just passed. So I stuck my head into the shaft, waited a little for my eyes to adjust to the darkness of the cellar, and saw my assumption confirmed. Now I quickly looked for a container and then lowered myself down over the coal chute into the cellar. I quickly shovelled a couple of shrivelled potatoes into the small dented tin bucket and almost could not get out of the high shaft hole. I was only able to pull myself up with the greatest of efforts.

When I got back to my company I whispered into Hans' ear that he should start a fire. Fortunately he still had matches that he had wrapped in foil. In addition to a mess kit, usually a tin can, each prisoner also carried a small bundle of sticks with them. Once you found something to eat you could cook it immediately without causing a fuss. Preparation and consumption are as inconspicuous as possible in order to protect yourself from having it snatched out of your mouth. Hans made a modest fire, I piled up three potatoes with a little water in the can, and we waited with anticipation for the meal. After the little refreshment the order came again to continue our march.

We soon came through a wooded area, next to which a stream flowed, over which small bridges ran at intervals. My buddy Hans and I decided to separate ourselves from the company and make our way through the woods on our own. By doing this we hoped to gain our freedom. Unfortunately for us, a Russian guard who had accompanied another company and was now returning got in our way. He had a machine gun with him and ordered us to stop. Then he searched us, but found nothing. When I noticed that he was raising his machine gun to shoot us, I shouted desperately with my hands in the air: 'Stoi pan', meaning 'Stop, sir!' I had something that we could exchange for our lives. I had sewn a new manicure set into the lining of my trousers. So I moved this case out with my finger. The Russian had in the meantime put his machine gun down. I showed him the brand-new parts and how they worked. The Russian clearly took a liking to it, gave us both a hard kick on the behind, and let us go. If he had been a wretch he still would have killed us. This time our life depended on a manicure set and a moment of human emotion.

With the greatest caution we stalked our way to the next bridge, which we first hid ourselves under. We had decided to wait for the next Austrian company. When it came we introduced ourselves to the sergeant and asked him to take us with him. He pulled out a list, checked our names, and took us in. We were lucky because this sergeant was a clever chap. On the way he told us to take a seat at the foot of a hill and explained his plan to us. He was convinced that we would not be released but that we would be dragged off to Russia. He also knew the area well and knew that all bridges had been destroyed as far as the town of Lundenburg/Břeclav on the border with Lower Austria. He wanted to lead us to freedom: to do this he demanded discipline from us, which meant marching in an orderly fashion with the Austrian flag held high at the head of our group, and when he gave the order we were to start to march in parade step. If the Russians stopped us on the way, he would explain to them that he had been instructed to lead the company from Brünn to Vienna for a work assignment.

There were three days of forced marching to the Austrian border, and again and again someone was left behind exhausted along the way. Late in the evening of the second day, when to make matters worse it was raining, we looked for shelter in a brick factory. Hans and I were able to save just enough dry wood from the rain for a fire to cook the last three potatoes in our tin can. With that our last bit of food was used up. After a short break we had to march on at two o'clock in the morning. Before we set off the sergeant told us that we had to march through Lundenburg on this last forced march. There was no other way. The sergeant encouraged us that we would make it and would reach freedom that same day.

Hunger and the strains of the last while were so draining that I felt unable to cope with this upcoming feat of strength without food. It was a nagging thought so close to freedom. I felt like I was near the end.

On the morning of the day of judgement, around six or seven o'clock, we passed through a small village. I absolutely had to get myself something to eat here, otherwise it would be all over for me. I still had my watch sewn into my cap. I ran into a house with my watch in hand, showed it to people, and gestured towards my mouth with my other hand. They understood that I wanted to trade it for food. The man tore open the kitchen cupboard, took out a loaf of bread about 40 centimetres in diameter, and came up to me. Then his wife intervened, tore the loaf from the man's hand, and gave me a much smaller piece of bread instead. In contrast to his wife the man had a kind heart; he reached onto the upper shelf and quickly pushed a piece of bacon into my hand. It all happened in a very short time. With a cry of thanks on my lips I stormed out of the door and panted after my company. Now Hans and I had at least a few more bites to survive the day.

In the morning at around ten o'clock on 20 May 1945 – Pentecost Sunday – we finally reached Lundenburg. The place was full of Russian soldiers. We marched through the streets in a parade-like manner: flag ahead, eyes left or right when ordered if a Russian officer was to be saluted. It was really exhausting. Nobody stopped us, so we looked organized. We came to the first bridge that crossed the river Thaya/Dyje. There was a Russian sentry there who asked for papers, so we turned left and came to the second bridge, where there was another sentry. At the third – the Post Bridge – our sergeant explained in Russian as we were approaching that we had the order to march to Vienna. The guard shouted: '*Davai!*' ('Carry on!'), and let us pass. We crossed the river and continued marching.

It was now 2pm and there were still 5 kilometres to go to the border. As there were guaranteed to be Russian border guards there we took a dirt road and marched into the first Austrian village of Bernhardsthal. Shortly before we had passed a road sign saying that Mistelbach near Vienna was 30 kilometres away. We marched in an orderly fashion through the village with the flag in front and found that it was entirely in Russian hands. Locals were wearing white armbands. At around 5pm, after we had crossed the village unchecked and were in an open field, we finally took our first break. The sergeant warned us that we should not stay here long: it was too dangerous. He also advised us not to go to Salzburg or Vienna and to march at least in pairs but not in groups of any more than five. The sergeant was a great guy, and finally he also gave us tips on how to find our way using the constellations in the night sky.

As the sergeant was giving us the last pieces of advice, we heard noises. There were about forty Czech police officers rolling up to us on rickety bicycles. With their guns at the ready, they ordered us to put our hands up and asked for the leader of the troops. Our sergeant reported immediately and stubbornly declared that he had been assigned to take us to Vienna. But it was no use: we had to go back to Bernhardsthal. There our sergeant was grilled for over an hour by the Russians, as he later told us. In the meantime we begged the local population for something to eat. I will never forget the kindness of these people. They took the last of their cans and provisions from the cellar for us. The family that I begged from quickly put on a saucepan full of potatoes, and after a long time we could once again eat our fill.

Then came the Russian order we already knew about and we had to go back down the road that had almost led us to freedom. We arrived in Lundenburg at midnight. We would have liked to have rested here, as we were soaked from the rain. Instead, we got a few hard kicks on the backside and had to march for another three hours. It had stopped raining, but we were wet to the bone. The night was cold and we shivered relentlessly. At three o'clock that night we arrived in a small town. If we did not find a dry place now then we were going to die, that was clear to us, so we immediately started to look around. We soon discovered a stately building with archways that must have burned down only a few days earlier.

Steps led down into the building, and soldiers crouched down everywhere. A little further below we saw a small light. We worked our way forward, stepping over the bodies of the resting men, and saw a candle standing on a window ledge that dimly lit the surroundings. Soldiers lay all over the place lined up like sardines; it seemed to be overcrowded everywhere. Then our gaze fell onto a corner where there was no one. We headed for the spot and discovered that there were six or seven charred corpses lying there. I said to my comrade: 'Hans, those are just charred corpses, the dead can't harm us!' Then we levelled off their remains a little and lay down in the still warm ashes. So we gratefully spent the night in there. The people who had been burned probably saved our lives at that time.

Chapter Sixteen

Journey into captivity

Our journey into captivity continued at seven o'clock the next morning. On the way we had different guards – we were accompanied in relays, so to speak. There was nothing to eat, and we were all exhausted. My friend Hans had a blanket with him that had become very heavy from the rain, but we did not want to leave it behind under any circumstances. So we got ourselves a branch, put the wet blanket over it, and took turns in carrying it. Again and again we also had to give each other support. I noticed that Hans was even worse off than me: his feet were also bleeding.

We stopped in Pressburg, present-day Bratislava. We were taken to the football stadium and were to spend the night there. It was incredibly draughty and we were all wet. I knew that if I could not find a dry place to stay, it would mean certain death for Hans, who was becoming ever more apathetic. I begged him to keep going while I looked around for a dry place for the night. In certain places inside here you were allowed to move about freely. Soon I discovered a man-made piece of elevated land behind a wooden fence. It must have been a machine-gun post, I thought to myself. I tried to get there, and had to crawl through a dirty channel. It was indeed a former machine-gun post. With my strength dwindling, I dug out the dirt, dug a hole in the ground, and then tore a few slats off the fence so that I could make a fire for ourselves afterwards. Hans still had some matches. Now all I had to do was get him. I found Hans collapsed on the ground. Prisoners who were also lying around exhausted on the ground were already being shot further up. I spoke to Hans, but he did not respond. I desperately poked him in the ribs, yanked him up, and yelled at him: 'Hans, pull yourself together, I've found us something for the night.' He slowly came to, and with our last combined strength we made it to our shelter. Soon afterwards we had a soothing fire crackling. I placed the branch that we had dragged along across our shelter and put the blanket over it so it could dry out. At the same time it protected us from the night air. I kept adding more wood, and luckily it did not rain any more. Finally I fell asleep too. When I woke up the following morning I noticed that the sleeve of my coat was burned. I had not noticed anything as I slept. Hans had recovered somewhat and said that if I had not helped him, it would have been 'curtains' for him. He would definitely have been shot.

In Bratislava we were crammed into cattle trucks, and we were brought in these via Budapest to Focşani in eastern Romania. There was a prison camp here where German soldiers were being detained. Gypsies greeted us with their string instruments, but it was all of no interest to us; we did not care. After Focşani we arrived via Bucharest in Constanţa, a Romanian port city right on the Black Sea. It was the summer of 1945. The wagons were parked on the tracks of a narrow headland. This narrow strip was washed by the sea on both sides. Guards were posted on the landward side, and there was no chance of escaping. We now awaited our further fate. It was really hot: we were hungry anyway, but the thirst was almost unbearable. Most of the prisoners stayed in a hall because it was a little cooler there. I was out in the open pondering how to quench my indescribable thirst. Moaning did not help anyone, I just did not want to surrender myself to fate. That was not my style. My gaze fell on a cast-iron lid in the floor.

I already suspected that there was something underneath to refuel the wagons. With great difficulty I managed to get the lid up: underneath was a room about 2 metres by 2 with lots of pipes and taps. I climbed down, took hold of a pipe, and immediately felt the coolness of the water. I turned the tap on this pipe, and fresh, cool water immediately gushed over me. I quenched my thirst with indescribable pleasure, and washed and cooled my body. Then I went back up and got Hans so that he too could quench his thirst. Gradually the others started to come too. It looked like a stream of ants going up and down one after the other. The water gave life and hope once again. We stayed in Constanţa for two days and were able to observe a huge ship being loaded around the clock. Cranes heaved all sorts of things on board, including chairs and other pieces of furniture, basically everything that was not nailed down. The things came here from Germany and were being shipped. When everything was loaded, we too had to board the *Transsylvanya*, that was the name of the freighter. Then we sailed off.

Together with other prisoners we spent the journey across the Black Sea lying in an area of the hallway on deck. Not far from us was a small counter where food for the officers was collected from. Hans and I had been poking around near the counter the whole time, wondering how we could get something to eat ourselves. The serving of food was coming to an end. Now I asked Hans to hand me his mess kit, since I only had a tin can. Very slowly, staying the whole time on the ground, I moved closer to the counter. A Russian woman was giving out the portions at the counter. When I was sitting right under the counter, I looked at her with wide eyes. After making sure the other prisoners were not paying attention to me, I held the mess kit up to her. I asked her in Russian for something to eat. She looked at me, took the ladle, and poured me some soup. I thanked the woman, without making myself conspicuous of course, and returned to Hans. We were grateful for the warm soup in our stomachs. It did us good and made us feel that we could survive for a little while longer again.

Another time when I was looking around for something to eat on deck I saw a couple of covered sacks. I leaned against them very casually so that the guard would not get suspicious. Then I inconspicuously felt the sacks and made a small hole in one with my finger. Very slowly I took out the round, hard little balls and let them slide into my trouser pocket. It was peas. However, I could not eat more than a dozen of these dry, hard things in one go. As always I shared these with Hans.

We were disembarked in Novorossiisk, a Russian port city in the Krasnodar region. As we crossed the city the people let us feel their hatred. We got spat on and some got kicked in the rear end. We marched uphill through a narrow valley, and were told to sit down on a hill, from where we could no longer see the city. Guards were posted all around. The hunger made itself felt the whole time. We did not get anything to eat.

As always we had a bundle of sticks and wood with us. But where would we get something edible here? There was no house to be seen far and wide, all around was just nature. I noticed the many hazelnut bushes. Then it occurred to me that this was a place where snails liked to go. I did not hesitate long: I sat down under a bush and began carefully and as inconspicuously as possible to dig for snails in the foliage. If the others had noticed that there might be something to eat here they would have pounced on it immediately. I actually found two snails. I brought these to Hans. I returned to the bushes and found six more, which also secretly went into the mess kit. Unfortunately Hans made a grievous error. He had a little salt and had already salted the snails while they were still cooking: it made the animals tough as leather, but we ate them anyway.

We wondered what our captors were up to up here. And we feared that they wanted to starve us and then shoot us. In the afternoon it was the same again: '*Davai, davai!*' We went back down to Novorossiisk, where we were loaded into cattle trucks. But before we got in we had to block up all the windows with barbed wire. For this I had to go and get wooden slats together with a Russian guard. On the way we passed a pitiful ammunition magazine, and on its ramp I discovered a smashed barrel with a thick white mass pouring out of it. When we passed it on the way back I saw a woman gathering up what had spilled out. I asked her to give me some of it. I held out my cap and she tossed in a handful of the spilled curd. I might be repeating myself, but I was grateful for every kind of meal. It is hard to imagine today: plagued by constant hunger, getting food had become our *raison d'être*.

We were crammed into the cattle trucks like sardines. In the middle of the floor there was an opening of about 20 square centimetres, which served as a latrine, or the quiet place as the soldiers called it. Whoever had to lie beside it really had bad luck. I had had this experience myself on the journey from Bratislava to Constanţa. We were lying so close together that I was repeatedly pushed to the edge of the latrine. Many prisoners had diarrhoea, and the stench of this and the dirt that you inevitably ended up with yourself were anything but pleasant.

We prisoners were housed in here in three layers. The lower tier was the floor of the wagon with the latrine in the middle, the upper two floors consisted of bunks. You could only lie sideways everywhere because you were cooped up so tightly; turning around was a laborious affair and only worked if everyone in the row lay down on the same side at the same time. I was not the only one who almost died on the journey. The bunks along with the prisoners on them above my spot would have crashed down on me once if I had not noticed their wretched state and prevented it by supporting them in good time. The destination of our journey was a prison camp in the Russian city of Tuapse, about 130 kilometres south of Novorossiisk on the Black Sea coast. I cannot say how long our trip lasted, but it was definitely longer than a week. In any case we got there on 13 August 1945.

Chapter Seventeen

The struggle for survival

Compared to the approximately 1,000 inmates in the camp, we were still almost 'fresh'. The prisoners in here were totally apathetic, and moved absent-mindedly through the camp. They were also unshaven and had a rash like lepers. We newcomers were housed in a strange room that had most likely been previously used as a theatre: a kind of revolving stage suggested this. Some slept up there on wooden bunks, the rest of us down in the room. There was not even straw on the dirty, hard bunks, and when you came into the room in the evening you could hear the bugs creeping about. At night these little monsters would then crawl over the exhausted and emaciated bodies of the prisoners to get their meal of blood. Some men were spared, but they seemed to like my blood particularly well. In the mornings I looked almost like a Mongolian, my face was so swollen.

We had to work in the quarry and cut wood. The strenuous work and malnutrition drained our emaciated bodies, and many lay around on the bare ground from exhaustion. It was raining, the ground was damp, and for many of them their strength was at an end. Every morning I counted eight to ten dead people being carted away and buried. I was already figuring out when it would happen to me too. Not only hunger and exhaustion were to blame for death. The cold, damp ground did the rest for many. I did not want to wait idly for my end and had to come up with something. So I scraped the mortar off a brick wall with a nail to get to the bricks. I succeeded. I stacked three of them on top of each other and from then on I had a dry seat – at night I slept sitting on it. I slept this uncomfortable way for five weeks. I was very rigid when I got up in the morning, and I felt dizzy every time I got up.

Once I was assigned to do woodwork, and a Romanian injured my finger with a wooden stick, so I was allowed to stay in the camp for a few days. It was a welcome break from work during which I could relax a little. After my recovery I had to help build a wall at the port of Tuapse. The ground was already frozen and we had to go to work barefoot every day. Sooner or later that was going to be fatal, so I thought about how to get some footwear. With a hatchet that I borrowed from a Russian I chopped up two wooden boards to make soles. I pulled so many threads out of a rubber tube that I could use them to braid two loops. I attached these to the soles with bent wire clips. Thus at least I had something like sandals and no longer had to walk around barefoot, and I could at least protect my feet from direct contact with the cold icy ground.

One day, as it was already approaching the winter of 1945, the few Austrians were brought together in the camp and divided into two groups. My friend Hans was one of the group of prisoners who were in very poor physical condition and were therefore released from captivity. We parted ways here, because I was then relocated with the rest of the Austrians towards the Turkish border. Our destination was prison camp no. 333/2 in Hadachin in the Caucasus, south of the highest mountain in Russia, Mount Elbrus.

Postcard sent by Raffeiner from Russian captivity in Hadachin (Georgia). On the front the Red Cross camp number was noted in Russian (333/2), thus the relatives did not know where the prisoner was.

We were transported in open trucks, and there was nothing to eat. On the way the vehicle stopped once under a wild pear tree. I climbed onto the roof of the driver's cab to be able to reach the pears and stuffed every pocket of my clothes full with them. When I got down again, most of the rest had already been stolen from me. The pears were so sour that they make your mouth pucker, but they were welcome food.

When we arrived at our destination in October 1945 there was no food for us as we had hoped. No, instead we were taken straight to the railway station, where we first had to unload bricks. The bricks were carried over a kind of chute that ran from the train to the ground. It was me of all people who had to pick them up off the ground and pass them on. The others could pass the bricks while standing, but I had to bend down first with each one. After a short time I became really dizzy. I could not keep up this work for long. Then I found a wooden stick that I could push under the chute so that I could get the bricks at stomach height. I interrupted the flow of work to get this block of wood, but straight away a German guard started yelling at me. He reproached me for thinking that I could stop the whole process. Prisoners were also chosen to supervise the others, often leaders with the rank of sergeant, lieutenant or other officer. That had already been the case in Tuapse, but there I had found the German officers to be more restrained. But this one here, who had once held the rank of paymaster, seemed on the other hand to want to make a real name for himself. That a man from my own ranks, who was nothing more than a prisoner himself, behaved like that was too much for me at that moment. I lost my temper and yelled at him: 'You're a wretch! First you officers all ran us into the hell of the front line until the very last day, and now you want to save your own life on the back of our misery!' This was all true, but I knew right away that this guy would have me in his sights from now on. For the next few days I tried to get away from this drudgery of loading bricks. Most of the prisoners could only last a week doing this work. I learned that the prisoners had set up a small factory here: a carousel lathe was used to make propellers for ships, and they were still looking for mechanics there. I immediately got in touch and got the job. Close to the factory was the barracks for the fifteen or so German officers and lieu-tenants who coordinated the work in the camp on behalf of the Russians. The very next day I reported for my new job in the factory. When my name was called during the roll call and I answered, a little lieutenant looked at me and said: 'Ah, so you're Raffeiner, you won't be with us for long!'

I did not feel well any more, and now I was in a right mess. The word about my verbal faux pas at the train station had got around, and it was precisely those who it had been aimed at that now partly determined my future fate. Now things could only go downhill. I actually only stayed in the factory for a few days, then I was again forced to unload bricks at the railway station. Still, the short time in the factory had not been in vain. I had snatched whatever had been lying around and could be pocketed: here a pathetic little flat-nose pliers, there a piece of wire or a small steel tube, a broken saw blade; I was even able to steal a small gun cartridge. I hoped to be able to make useful things with these that I could exchange for something edible. This was not wishful thinking: in the evenings I had watched other prisoners busily tinkering about in the barracks. I was sure they were not doing this just to pass the time. My assumption was soon confirmed. But as a precaution I buried my 'loot' so that it could not be stolen from me: I walked thirty paces in a straight line from the barracks to the corner post and buried the cartridge and the other things there.

The year 1945 passed and spring was now approaching. Our camp was separated by a wooden wall from the sub-camp, where Ukrainian prisoners were being held. There was, however, a place where a few loose boards could be moved to be able to slip through. That was the passage-way to the bartering in the neighbouring camp. You had to be very careful because there were guards in both camps. Another way to barter was on the long road to work. It took a good three-quarters of an hour to walk from the camp to the station, and we returned to the camp at noon and in the evening. Along this road we met Russian women's brigades. These women were there as forced labour, but I did not know the reasons for this. Once along the way I saw a Ukrainian selling a Russian woman a needle for 5 rubles. That spurred on my ambition – I too wanted to sell needles. But seeing that I did not have any needles, I had to make some myself. In order to do this I sneaked into the Ukrainian camp during the night and looked for things that might be of use. I found a steel cable that I took a piece of wire out of, and I tried to make needles from this. The shape was not the problem: the hardest part was the eye of the needle because it kept breaking off. Out of ten attempts, only three needles were usable, but I was already looking forward to my earnings. But I could forget getting 5 rubles. I got 2 rubles for the first needle and had to hawk each additional needle for only 1 ruble each. The quality of my homemade needles was just not as good as the real ones. When I finally got my 5 rubles I was able to buy a slice of bread. It was about 10 by 10 centimetres. This piece of bread was incredibly valuable to me, and I savoured it bite by bite.

Other prisoners, who had to chop wood in the forest and make tiles, made wooden toys. They sold the toys in passing to the Russian women, who in turn sold them in the villages.

Before I started earning my extra income with the needles I had tried other ways too. The camp was teeming with mice, and nothing was safe from the countless voracious rodents. But the mice were not only annoying, they were also carriers of diseases. One day we were told: 'Whoever brings thirty dead mice will get a ladle of soup!' This very attractive offer came from the German paymaster, the same guy whom I had called a wretch down at the harbour. I did not think much of it and went straight to work making a mousetrap. I took a small piece of wood and bent a bracket and a spring from a piece of solid wire. Soon the trap was ready for use. A piece of bread served as bait, then I set the trap up, and before I had even left it snapped shut. Catching mice worked wonderfully. I caught thirty mice in one night, and I was looking forward to the extra portion of soup. But instead of the promised soup I only got a malicious grin from the German paymaster, who said: 'Haha, you thought you were going to get a drop of soup?' That was like a slap in the face! Hatred rose up in me. I had been blacklisted since the incident at the station, and the guard took every opportunity to harass me and to order me around.

I had far fewer problems with the Russian guards. On the contrary: once, while I was on my way to the outhouse, I begged an elderly Russian guard for a cigarette. 'Sit down,' he replied in Russian. Then he took tobacco and newspaper out of his jacket pocket and started rolling a cigarette. He asked where I came from.

'*Austriski*,' I told him.

'Where in *Austriski*? Bozen?'

'Yes,' I replied surprised. The Russian now told me that he had been imprisoned in Neumarkt/Egna south of Bozen during the First World War and had suffered terrible hunger. He wanted to tell more about his involuntary stay in South Tyrol, but another Russian guard interrupted our conversation and chased me away. Unfortunately, I never met the older Russian again.

There was only one officer in the camp who treated me even-handedly and humanely. He was the senior physician who was in charge of the infirmary. I was once declared unfit for work because of severe jaundice. When I had to go to the senior physician about it he told me he had nothing to give me, just some tea made from herbs that the prisoners had collected. The illness really affected me; I was particularly miserable and felt very weak. The hunger gnawed at my intestines and the disease consumed me.

When I was not sleeping in my bunk in the infirmary I observed everything that was going on around me. Thus I noticed that not only the bloody, purulent bandages and other unsavoury rubbish were disposed of in the latrine, but a box was also emptied every day at lunchtime. When you are constantly hungry you almost develop a sixth sense of where to find something to eat. I was right in my assumption that it could possibly be waste from the infirmary kitchen. When I crept to the latrine the following evening I found in this literal dirt potato skins and even a few small potatoes, which I immediately boiled and ate. I felt no horror, and yet I could not help thinking of the prisoner at Uman who had attacked the stinking remains of a horse carcass like an animal. Now I had reached this point myself.

Chapter Eighteen

A research hospital?

The jaundice, as badly as it consumed me, turned out in retrospect to be a stroke of luck for me. I would almost call it a kind of heavenly intervention, because when I was once visiting the senior physician at the beginning of the illness the Russian pharmacist came by. I do not know whether he was really a pharmacist, but that was what he was known as. During the conversation between the two of them the pharmacist took out an American tin can and gesticulated around with it. I saw perplexity written on the senior physician's face and asked him what the pharmacist wanted. So he told me he had to look for someone who could make a lid for the tin can for him. That was an assignment for me, and I said this to him, but I would need a second tin can. The pharmacist agreed, and after two days I handed over the can and lid, which I had burned dark in the fire and which had an almost artistic appearance to it. As a reward I got a bowl of soup.

I also made a second lid for the pharmacist. As he was testing the little work of art, the senior Russian camp physician came in. She saw the lid and asked who made it. The pharmacist pointed to me. The two talked and then I was asked if I could make a padlock for the senior physician. That was a challenge. I went to the door for a moment and wondered how I could do it. Finally I accepted the task. It was necessary, however, for the doctor to accompany me to the Ukrainian camp so that I could get the proper material. There I got myself a car door, a steel cable, and a piece of wire, and then I got to work. Since I was constantly being ordered about by the German paymaster during the day, I was only able to put my project into practice in the evening without any interference. After four days I had the padlock ready. The doctor tried the lock out again and again, and she openly showed me her delight at it. I got the order to make more locks. A lock every four days, that was our agreement. During this time, however, I managed to make two of them, and I was able to offload the second in the Ukrainian camp. As a reward I was allowed to slip into the Ukrainian camp every day at evening time and get a piece of bread there. This daily piece of bread strengthened my body, but also my soul.

Incidentally, my jaundice had been discovered during the so-called 'meat inspection'. This is what we called the monthly rounds of a medical team that decided who was considered fit for work. The criteria for this were not always clear to me: in addition to our state of health, the mood of the doctors probably also played a role. When my jaundice had more or less subsided, I was promptly discharged. That meant that the doctors had found me fit for work again. When I came out from my check-up the pay-master was waiting outside and commented on my having been discharged with a broad grin: 'So, Raffeiner, tomorrow it's back to work. We'll get you over to where the others are!' While saying this he held out his hand in the direction where the dead were buried. I felt a sense of unease rising in me. Could I have been mistaken? Had the senior doctor forgotten me? She had promised to stand up for me so that I could stay in the camp. If I got reassigned to the work brigade then I would be at the mercy of the paymaster. I knew what that meant for me. I was almost unable to sleep that night, these thoughts tormented me.

The next morning I hid under my bunk. Outside, the work brigade had lined up for roll call. Suddenly I heard the paymaster yelling my name out loud: 'Raffeiner!' It reverberated around inside me. Now I had no other choice: I had to step forward for better or for worse. When the paymaster saw me, he yelled at me: 'You really think you can hang around here in the camp for another month? Fall in immediately!' So I lined up with the brigade and thought: 'So, now you're done for!' Then the line of people trotted off to go to work at the railway station. After about a hundred metres some Russians came towards us, including the senior Russian physician. She saw me, stopped, and shouted to me in a command-like fashion that I had to report to her at noon. After the grind at the railway station we marched back to the camp. I went to see the senior physician immediately, and she angrily asked me why I had gone to work. I told her how everything had happened, after which she dismissed me with a '*Davai!*' I did not know what to do and moped around watching. Then I noticed the paymaster also going in to see the senior doctor. When he came out after about five minutes he seemed dejected to me. After a short time the doctor called me again. This time she welcomed me kindly and informed me that I was allowed to stay in the camp and that I was to continue making locks for her. She also assured me that the paymaster would leave me alone in future and that I could move freely around the camp. I was naturally very happy. I immediately fetched my tools, looked for a nice spot in the warm April sun, and got to work – my mood shone along with the sun as if they were racing one another.

I was more than happy with the way things were going, and my technical skills had secured a little quality of life for me under completely unfortunate circumstances. Then the following misfortune happened to me. Like every day, I was doing my usual work when a splinter hit me in the eye while I was chiselling. My eye became infected, I developed a fever, and probably lost consciousness for a few days. There was nothing in the prison camp with regard to medical care. As little as my jaundice was treated, no one could help me this time either, except that my eyes were bandaged with a rag. I had both eyes bandaged because even the healthy eye could no longer tolerate the light. The senior Russian doctor looked after me and made sure that I was transferred to the camp hospital in Krasnodar, and she accompanied me there personally. When we got to town at the end of April 1946 we travelled by tram for a while, and then she led me the rest of the way. In front of the hospital she told me to sit down and wait for her. Then I heard a man's voice. He said that luckily I only had an eye injury because there was nothing they could do about it here in the hospital. I did not understand, because we had come with the intention of getting better care for me here. He observed that this was a research hospital and strongly urged me to be careful. I was not to report anything about my previous illnesses or those of my parents, because experiments were being carried out on people here. He also suggested that I hand my belongings over to him, he would keep them for me for the time being. My curiosity had grown so strong by now that I lifted the rag up from over my healthy eye. I blinked a little and saw a barbed-wire fence in front of me. Behind it stood a gaunt chap dressed only in ragged underpants. I wondered if I could trust him. I had packed up my belongings in a piece of blue apron material: my Italian *congedo*, a small evangelical field hymn book, a postal savings book that only contained the last page, a spoon that I had made myself, and a set of rosary beads. I rated the likelihood that I would not get my things back after the visit to the doctor higher than that the guy behind the fence would hold on to them for me.

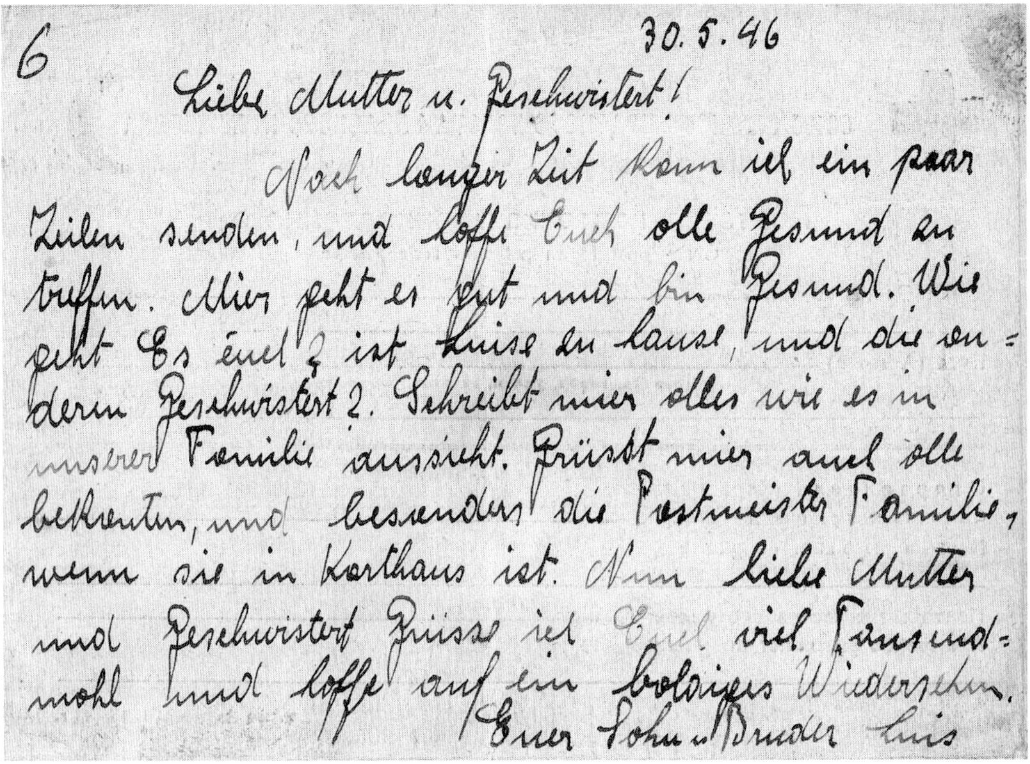

30. 5. 46

Liebe Mutter u. Geschwistert!

[handwritten letter in German cursive, partially legible]

‘I'm doing fine and am healthy.’ Due to the censoring of post the actual situation could not be disclosed. Postcard from captivity to Raffeiner's mother and siblings. 30 May 1946.

So I threw my package over the barbed wire to him. After a while my senior Russian physician came back and took me to the sentry post at the entrance, where she dropped me off. She said goodbye in a friendly manner and even thanked me for my work. She expected that I would be back soon – she gave me this feeling. Could I have been mistaken?

Everything I was wearing was taken from me in the hospital. Now I was just standing there in my underpants or what was left of them. As far as my few belongings were concerned, I had made the right decision. The guy was from Vienna and was an honest person; he gave everything back to me.

The atmosphere in this place was anything but inviting. I slept only in my underpants in a wooden bunk with no straw or other type of bedding. During the day the inmates also lay around on the wooden steps. You did not have to work, and you moved as little as possible so as not to use up unnecessary calories. Every now and then the doctor would come and choose one of the inmates to bring with her. Not infrequently the patient never came back. The severity of their illness was not necessarily a selection criterion: it was rumoured in here that these people were passed on to hospitals for medical experiments. That is why the man from Vienna had immediately warned me not to mention any illnesses in my family if asked about them. His warning prompted me to take my bandage off after a short time in the hospital, even though my inflamed eye was still quite sensitive to light and was sore. I was afraid of ending up as a guinea pig. And he seemed to be right, because even though I was brought in for my eye injury, no one had treated me yet. Over time the pain became more bearable, but I saw almost nothing out of that eye any more.

Nevertheless I felt like a guinea pig, especially regarding the question of how little food humans can survive on. For breakfast and dinner we were given a slice of bread that was 10 by 7 centimetres and 5 millimetres thick, plus a glass of rosehip tea. At lunchtime there was always some kind of soup. This consisted of exactly five tablespoons of soup and one table-spoon of filler, either millet or noodles or barley. When serving out the portions every spoonful was meticulously smoothed out. I could not imagine that this effort was made simply because the food was scarce or that there was an excessive sense of justice. Some inmates even suspected that chemical substances were mixed in with the meals. They explained it by saying that they were suffering from memory lapses that they had never noticed before. For me too this diet was not without its effects. I was getting progressively thinner, and I honestly have to admit: I could not remember my own father's name at all. But I do not know whether that was due to any substances or to the meagre food.

One day the doctor came and called my name. I got a fright, but I had no choice but to go with her. We entered a two-storey building and went to a dental treatment room. An old worn-out dentist's chair stood in the middle of the room, and there were also a few young girls – who to my mind were still minors. I was asked to sit on that disgusting chair. Then my details were recorded. My teeth were in terrible condition, and I was expecting the worst. The girls were getting dental training here, and we prisoners served as objects for training purposes. We were tangible teach-ing material. Suddenly a voice came from outside. At that same moment the doctor and the girls left everything and disappeared. Someone had called for dinner. I breathed a sigh of relief and disappeared as well. I was not called up again. Every time the doctor approached I turned my face away and pretended to be asleep. That is how I got away with it time and again.

Chapter Nineteen

Free at last

It was shortly before 15 August 1946. With writing utensils in her hands – it was actually only a piece of bark and a piece of coal – the doctor strolled through the camp. She kept making notes. It soon turned out that all Austrians were written down, but I found out that I was not on the list. My comrade from Vienna was lying next to me and I asked him to ask the doctor why I was not written down. She replied that I was a *Nemetski*, that is, a German. 'No, *Austriski*,' he retorted, I was Austrian. I confirmed this to her. Nevertheless she insisted that I was German, but we on the other hand reiterated our assertion. It went back and forth like this, and then she left. When she came back she asked me to go with her. She had convinced herself that our assertion was correct. Now I was taken to the general practitioner, who read my medical history and examined my injured eye. I was put on the doctor's list, my hair was cut, and I was even allowed to bathe.

I was given clean bandages for both of my eyes and I was guided along when necessary. I also received a coat in the middle of August. My arms and body were far too thin to fill it, but I did not care. Everything happened in just a few hours when suddenly all Austrians were gathered together to leave. We were indeed set free. We were taken to the exit, where a guard took us over. In the meantime I had pushed up the bandage over my healthy eye so that I could see. They were all deteriorated physi- cally: even the boys had become old men. First we drove to Rostov-on- Don, where the local railway station was in the middle of the forest. We spent the night next to the tracks. The next morning around nine o'clock the train arrived. The journey went via Rostov to Vienna. Before we got there each of us was given a whole loaf of bread. It was amazing: a loaf of bread for everyone! The Russians wanted to demonstrate that the prisoners had enough to eat. In Vienna we were handed over to the Austrians.

We were housed in a school in the Hütteldorf district for the time being, and we were given food in a brewery that was located behind a park. This park was beautifully laid out, and there were many benches to relax on. But there was also a crowd of people: women and girls were walking around with posters. They had photos attached to them with the names and details of their missing sons, husbands or fathers. Again and again you were asked if you knew the missing person. I was sitting on a bench in the park when someone tapped me on the shoulder from behind. 'I know you,' I heard someone say. I turned around, but did not know the man. He told me that in Tuapse he always handed out the bread. I was glad that he had recognized me. He said he did not live far from there and invited me to go along with him. We were allowed to move about freely, and so I went with him. I stayed for dinner, and we had a lot to talk about. Although he certainly did not have much for himself he served up plum dumplings for me. That was a festive aroma! They were so delicious that I ate four of them. Afterwards we chatted on until around three in the morning. Then it began: my stomach was not used to the food and it rebelled. I did not want to let on anything, so I said goodbye with the excuse that it was already very late. I did not get far. I had such a stomach-ache that I rolled around in the gutter. The bloating and cramps were so severe that I thought it was going to tear me apart. 'So, that's it, now it's over,' I thought. After all that I had survived, was I now to have to die here in the gutter because of a few plum dumplings?

After a two-hour fight during which my stomach had relieved itself in every possible way I slowly began to feel better. That was a lesson for me. There was only a small portion of meagre soup for breakfast at the brewery. That was just right for our emaciated stomachs. There were those who, like me, had stuffed themselves full and had genuinely ended up dying in the process. Nevertheless we were happy when the population provided us with food. The people did not have much of their own, yet many shared the little they had with us. Once a man came in with a back-pack that had lots of steam coming out of it. Even before he opened it the smell of boiled potatoes filled our noses. They were divided out as far as they would go. Such gestures of sympathy filled us with gratitude and I at least would never forget them.

After a few days in Vienna we first drove to Linz, and from there we arrived at the Reichenau camp in Innsbruck. The discharge centre for returnees was housed there. I had had to leave my homeland almost seven years previously: on 19 September 1946 I was officially released from military service here. Now I stood there as a free man and wondered what I should do next. During a period of leave in 1944 I had visited Marianne Grüner, Bernhard's sister, and her family in Lienz in East Tyrol. Marianne worked for a mechanic in his home. We had agreed at the time that I would come to Lienz after the war had ended and that she would then ask about a job for me with this mechanic. I wanted to go there now. Before that, I drove to my base in Inzing in the Oberinntal, where I wanted to get my suit I had left there. Unfortunately the suit had been stolen from the closet. I did not want to turn up at Marianne's looking as scruffy as I did, so I wrote to her that I would go home to my mother and sister and would not come until spring. Next I applied to the Red Cross to enter South Tyrol – I was still a German citizen after all. I waited in vain for over a month for the permit. Then I decided to travel illegally over the mountains to South Tyrol.

At the end of October I walked across the Similaun mountain into the Schnalstal. My mother and sister Maria were delighted to see me return, and I lived with them in the apartment in the post office. In the village few people took notice of my return. Every now and then I heard: '*Bisch a wieder do?*' ('Are you back again?') When I met my friend Bernhard for the first time and told him that I was back, he just muttered some incomprehensible remarks and left. Bernhard's fanaticism had destroyed our friendship. He himself was no longer happy, and he increasingly got into difficulties, and only came to me when he was looking for help from me.

In January 1947 my mother died. Now it was even easier for me to put my decision into practice. My hopes for the future and also my heart had remained in East Tyrol, and I had decided to return there.

All winter long my sister Maria had sewn together trousers and jackets for me from military clothing, shirts from sheets, and even a large backpack from a tarpaulin. I was getting myself ready for spring. I planned to move to East Tyrol as soon as the weather and road conditions over the mountains improved.

I got myself ready a package weighing around 25 kilograms neatly wrapped in packing paper that I stowed my belongings in. When the snow had started to melt in spring I ventured my first attempt to travel with such a heavy load in my backpack. I had underestimated the situation:

there was still too much snow and ice on the ground, and I had to turn back. I walked over the mountains six times in total until I had brought my belongings across the border – to be more precise to Vent in the Ötztal, because an acquaintance of mine from Schnals was working there for a farmer as a feeder. I could knock on his door at night too and hand over my things. He then handed in the parcels for me at the post office.

My sister Maria had decided to move in with our brother Peter on the Dorfmairhof in Naturns. I helped her take care of the household. It was June 1947 when I myself arrived in Vent with the last package and travelled on to East Tyrol. I was now living with the Grüner family, and I also got a job in Josef Thum's mechanic workshop.

In this post-war period there was great hardship everywhere. There was almost nothing to eat, and the ration cards were nowhere near enough. On weekends I always cycled across the countryside to beg the farmers for milk and food. The result was usually half a litre of milk and five or six potatoes.

Once, when we were going to work one morning, Marianne's mother said she did not know whether there would be something to eat for lunch. She just had nothing left. But then she managed to get hold of a few thin slices of polenta from a kind-hearted soul. That was the lunch for six people. With a hungry stomach I got up from lunch and had to go back to work.

Things did not go as I had imagined with Marianne either. I had long imagined that I would marry her and start a family with her. She was a nice, lovely girl and we had known each other since childhood. She had written to me often. She certainly liked me too, but the war had marked me and changed me. I noticed myself that I did not meet the expectations of a young woman. After all the hardships and experiences I no longer felt like a person, least of all a civilized one. So after three months in Lienz I decided to return to South Tyrol. Somewhere on a farm in my home country my artisan skills would definitely come in handy, and there was certainly no less to eat there than here.

Chapter Twenty

My new life

In September 1947 I returned to South Tyrol. For now I stayed with my siblings Peter and Maria in Naturns. I had hoped to meet Luise here too. After her training as a midwife in Karlsruhe, however, she had been sent to Yugoslavia. I had found out that after the front had collapsed there she had been given the task of taking around forty children from families who were *Donauschwaben* (Danube Swabians) – ethnic Germans (*Volksdeutsche*) who lived in the area between Hungary and Yugoslavia – to Carinthia in southern Austria on foot and by herself. Despite the fact that the Russian occupation forces had already moved forward, she had made it through their lines. But the children were too weak and she had to watch one child after another fall by the wayside and die. The agony of not being able to help these poor little things burned painfully in her soul for a long time. Luise stayed in the Sellraintal in Austria near our brother Toni, who was a shepherd all his life and remained single. My brother Sepp, on the other hand, had married. He had an accident as a young family man and left behind a wife with four children.

As for me, I had found accommodation with my siblings, but I still did not have regular work. With a friend I started repairing bicycles, but since there was hardly anything to be earned from it I smuggled lighters. I went over the approximately 3,500-metre Similaun in the Schnalstal to Vent in the Ötztal, bought lighters there, and sold them to a *carabiniere*. The Italian became a good customer because he also supplied his colleagues with my lighters.

I soon ventured into a far more difficult enterprise, but one that made me more money. I smuggled a motorcycle out of Switzerland. On the way there I went over the Reschenpass and noticed that the border was well manned with border police. So I decided to take another route home, quite a detour. Four friends from Schnals, who worked as shepherds in Vent, helped me carry the dismantled motorcycle across the Similaun into the Schnalstal. I kept the motorcycle for the time being. Only when I started to run out of money did I sell it. I soon decided to start my own business. I had my own tools, which I had bought in Lienz from what I earned in the Thum workshop. In Kompatsch, a village near Naturns, I rented a room that had previously been a wheelwright's workshop. So I continued to repair bicycles: I had plenty to do because there were not many cars at the time and the roads were full of holes and stones.

On Sundays I went to mass and then, like most men, to the inn. At first I remained an outsider. Even at the Catholic Men's Union, which I had joined, I did not really make any friends. As a native of Schnals I was considered an outsider in Naturns. Besides, I had been to the war and nobody wanted to talk about that. I mainly spent my free time in a familial environment with my cousin Peter and his wife Maria. Here I met Maria's sister Anna. I liked her and made inquiries about her from acquaintances, as was the custom at the time. I only heard praise and good things about her. That pleased and encouraged me at the same time. It turned out she liked me too, and we soon were making plans for the future together. I had found a wonderful girl, because I was gruff and quick-tempered at times. But she was by no means resentful, never nagged me, and she accepted me warts and all. We married in May 1949. Anna had been given a small piece of land next to her sister's farm, just big enough to build a small house on. I drew up the plans for our little house myself. With our own hands, with only the occasional help of a bricklayer, my wife and I finished our new home. We had to raise 500,000 liras for this. We exchanged a piece of land with my cousin Peter that Anna had got from her brother for the repayment of our loan. So now we were debt free, which was very important to both of us. But we also had to spend all our money for this to happen. When we moved in at Christmas 1949 we only had 2 liras left. After my time as a wheelwright I first worked as a machinist in the quartz quarry in Hilbertal near Plaus, which lies below Naturns, and then for a short time at the Trojer machine-fitter company in Meran. On the first day there the boss came to me and suggested that he had a 'job for life' for me. Just such a permanent position until retirement had been my wish. The master plumber at the Forst brewery in Algund/Lagundo had just died, so I went and introduced myself. After the trial period of twenty-four days I was permanently employed as a master plumber there and remained for twenty-five years – until my retirement on my 60th birthday.

My job was very interesting and diverse. When I started in 1952 beer-dispensing technology was not yet fully developed. I was often sent to inns because the beer foamed up far too much. Some bars even wanted to stop serving draft beer altogether as a result. An old German brewery law stated that the beer line was not allowed to be less than 10 millimetres in diameter, but I fiddled around and found that the beer flowed more steadily in a pipe 4 millimetres in diameter and no longer foamed up. Now it needed the right connections for this, which I made myself. Thus the problem was solved for the Algund brewery, and the installation of dispensing systems increased rapidly.

In the meantime I had become the father of two boys and two girls, so I was glad that in addition to my salary at the Forst company I was earning something extra so that the children could do an apprenticeship. I could make the connections I had invented myself outside of working hours – and they sold well. Soon I also invented the so-called drip trays. Up till then the beer just dripped onto the counter and had to be wiped away with a cloth the whole time. With the first models I was still drilling the holes manually. The brewery benefited greatly from these inventions. The dispensing columns supplied to the restaurants were not the result of my ingenuity, but instead of buying them from outside as before I was soon making them myself.

After my retirement the Forst brewery asked me to continue working for them. So I set up a small workshop in my garage and did fabrication work for the company in Algund. As I received more and more orders, my eldest son, who had also worked at the brewery, first got into the business, and later my second son too. In 1978 we founded the company Raffeiner Alois & Co. OHG. We had set up a new workshop, but after a while this too no longer met our needs with respect to orders. So we bought land in the industrial zone in Naturns and built a factory there. Gradually I withdrew from the business and left it to my two sons, and they continued it with great diligence. They now send delivery systems all over the world. I now had more time for my hobbies. When I was 48 I went skiing for the first time again after the war. This passion, like fishing and hiking, was something I still enjoyed in my old age. In the summer, on the other hand, the whole family went to the seaside, mostly on a camping holiday for three weeks. It was there that we got to know the Steffan couple from

Austria, with whom we often went together on holiday in the years that followed.

In addition to my work I also brought the benefits of my manual skills to the village community. I helped with the construction of the stage at the *Volksbühne* (national stage) in Naturns, because my wife Anna acted in the theatre there for years. Knowledge of my penchant for tinkering soon got around in the village, and Dean Georg Peer would ask me for my help with various projects in the parish. I also went on adventurous bicycle tours abroad with Peer or occasionally took part in his prayer evenings, which were based on those of the Taizé monastic order. Since I felt the need to get involved socially, I joined the local 'Third World Group' and took on a sponsorship for a mission project. In 1999 my wife Anna died, leaving a huge void in my life. I am grateful to my family, especially my two daughters, for the loving care, the time they devote to me, and the understanding that they show me. With this book my wish has come true that what happened will not be forgotten.

Afterword:
'Show your wound'

by Hannes Heer

Luis Raffeiner during the war

At the end of the story of his youth in the Schnalstal and the war in the Soviet Union Luis Raffeiner records how his life had changed. He will return to his homeland from East Tyrol. The woman whom he went to Lienz for after his return from captivity in 1947 will not become his wife or the mother of his children. 'She was a nice, lovely girl and we had known each other since childhood. She had written to me often. She certainly liked me too, but the war had marked me and changed me. I noticed myself that I did not meet the expectations of a young woman. After all the hardships and experiences I no longer felt like a person, least of all a civilized one' (see p. 150). Seldom has a former member of the Wehrmacht expressed so openly what had come back from the battles and massacres on the Eastern Front, what had come back home to civilian life and peaceful times from Hitler's race war and war of conquest – barbarians.

From his point of view everything had started so well after the Duce and the Führer had agreed that South Tyrol would remain Italian and that the German-speaking residents had to decide either to stay in the country or to emigrate to Germany. Raffeiner's family had 'like most other ordinary folk … gravitated towards the decision of educated people and those who were better off in the village' and opted for Germany. For him personally, too, that seemed to be the only right decision: 'I myself had nothing to lose at home because I did not own anything and had no job – things could actually only get better … One or two propaganda slogans had certainly left their mark in the back of my mind, but my decision was mainly based on the emotional level. Germany sounded more promising than Sicily, and I knew only too well what to expect from fascism' (see p. 30).

Leaving home, and the trip to the Brenner Pass and the border, became a folk festival. 'The people waved, the sheets fluttered, the heart eagerly awaited the unknown adventure. I was happy to be leaving' (see p. 31). And the entry into the Greater German Reich also began well – with a few rounds of free beer, paid for by the Gauleiter of Tyrol, Franz Hofer. Subsequent integration into the Wehrmacht turned out to be somewhat more difficult and was a sequence of mishaps and coincidences: a hernia and a stay in hospital during recruit training, not being there for the swearing of the oath to the Führer, and missing his first front-line deployment as a *Gebirgsjäger* in Norway in 1940. This resulted in Raffeiner training with the assault guns, a special unit in the Wehrmacht, and the postponement of his entry into the war for a year – until the attack on the Soviet Union on 22 June 1941.

The outline of a war

'Have you forgotten', wrote Frederick the Great in October 1773 to his friend Voltaire, 'that war is a scourge that throws all sorts of people together and also encourages all sorts of crimes?'[11] It may be that one can interpret a millennium of European wars using this phrase from the enlightened Prussian king, who had experience of war; but it failed for one war, the one from 1939 to 1945. This war was not a fate or a 'scourge', but a deliberate and long-prepared undertaking. It began on 3 February 1933, when Hitler, three days after his appointment as Reich Chancellor, explained his foreign policy programme to the commanders of the army and the navy: in order to militarize the people, all military shackles of the Versailles Treaty – primarily the prohibition of general conscription and the limitation of troop strength to 100,000 men – must be eliminated, and the Marxist-pacifist sentiment in Germany destroyed. 'Whoever does not want to be converted has to be broken ... Attitude of the youth and the whole people to the idea that only struggle can save us.' The long-term goal of his policy, as Hitler concluded, was the 'conquest of new *Lebensraum* [living space] in the East and its ruthless Germanization'.[12]

And it was also not a bunch of people 'thrown together' who attacked the neighbouring peoples of Europe from 1939 without a declaration of war, but the armed power of the German *Volksgemeinschaft* (national community), homogenized through the violent exclusion of all *Volksschädlinge* (public enemies) –Marxists, Jews, gypsies, gays, asocials, all those considered unworthy of life. Since the lightning victories achieved in the west, north and south-east of Europe in 1940 and 1941 at the latest, the Wehrmacht considered itself invincible and, like the majority of the German people, believed in the infallibility of the Führer, who had been sent by Providence.

After all, Hitler's war did not 'encourage all possible crimes', but its means as well as its end was criminality. This was especially true of the attack on the Jewish-Bolshevik Soviet Union. This struggle against the racial enemy and for living space in the east, according to Hitler, was a struggle for the fate of Germany and was therefore 'a just war'. It was therefore allowed to be conducted with all means available, including the most inhumane.[13] 'A sense of justice', as the Wehrmacht High Command translated this licence for the troops, had 'to give way to the necessity of war'.[14] The general orders that were given before the attack were issued accordingly. They are called 'the criminal orders' by historians:

- The political commissars were responsible for their 'barbaric Asiatic fighting methods' and would have to 'be dealt with immediately with a weapon'.[15] This introduced the murder of prisoners on the battlefield.
- Red Army prisoners of war should not be viewed as defeated 'comrades' but as opponents who had been educated to be 'mortal enemies of National Socialist Germany' and who had lost any 'right to treatment as an honourable soldier' required by international law.[16] This made the prisoners fair game.
- The civilian population was a haven of treachery, resistance, sabotage and betrayal, therefore the courts-martial common for civil offences were abolished: one could only defend oneself against the 'poison of decomposition' with a weapon in hand and defend oneself through 'collective violence'.[17] This opened a second front right from the beginning – the war against the civilian population.
- In the 'Guidelines for the conduct of troops in Russia', which had been handed to every soldier before the attack began, the enemy groupings of the coming war were named briefly and precisely: the

fight against Bolshevism required 'ruthless and energetic measures against Bolshevik agitators, irregulars, saboteurs, Jews'.[18] In addition to the struggle against possible partisans, these guidelines made the persecution of communists and Jews part of the military process.

These orders were based on three further directives. The first, which was to determine the fate of Soviet prisoners of war as well as that of the urban population, demanded that the Wehrmacht feed itself 'from the land' and send all surpluses back to Germany. According to the decision in Berlin on 2 May 1941 of the ministries involved, 'this will undoubtedly lead to the starvation of tens of millions of people'.[19] As a result of this decision 1 million Soviet prisoners of war died between July and December 1941.

The second, equally consequential, agreement was made between the Wehrmacht and the SS and provided for the formation of four SS *Einsatzgruppen* (task forces), which were to begin with the murder of the Jews behind the front. These groups operated according to Himmler's directives, but were 'subordinated to the Wehrmacht with regard to march orders, supply, and accommodation', and had to report all planned actions in good time.[20] The Wehrmacht expanded this agreed division of labour with extremely helpful preparatory measures: during the advance the Jews were registered, marked with yellow rags, and assigned to forced labour.[21] The third general decision concerned the targeted planning for the defeated Soviet Union: the living space in the east would serve as a supplier of food and as a colony of German settlers. In order to make room for this, a *Generalplan Ost* (General Plan East) commissioned by Himmler required 14 million local inhabitants to be allowed to live and be used as slave labour, but 31 million were to be deported and murdered.[22] Thus, every dead Russian was a piece of the German future.

But more decisive than these orders prepared in advance, agreements made and plans in progress, was whether it would be possible to convince the millions of soldiers in the armed forces that this programme of murder was to be the most just cause in the world. When writing *Mein Kampf*, Hitler had dealt extensively with the subject of propaganda and tried to explore how it could be used to generate 'a general conviction' of 'the necessity [and] the correctness' of a given process. The British approach in the First World War became his model. According to his conclusion, they had portrayed the Germans in advance as 'barbarians and Huns' and thus effectively prepared their own soldiers for the horrors of war: 'For the cruel effect of the weapon, which he was now already familiar with from the enemy, gradually appeared to him as proof of the 'Hun-like' brutality of the barbaric enemy, without ever being made to think for a moment that his own weapons ... could appear even more horrific.'[23]

Hitler applied this lesson when preparing the long-planned war against the Soviet Union. Determined to wage it outside the norms of international law, he made sure in his speeches, orders and instructions to conceal this scenario by branding his opponent as a lawbreaker. It was insinuated that the Soviet Union had planned an attack that the German Reich had only just pre-empted, that it was engaged in an 'Asiatic' way of fighting, and that it behaved outside any conventions of war and beyond all standards of a cultured nation: 'In the struggle against Bolshevism we cannot reckon with the behaviour of the enemy according with the principles of humanity or international law' became the key phrase of this diabolical propaganda ploy.[24] What was achieved with this demonization of the enemy was what was intended: convincing oneself of one's own just cause. The German way of waging war was evidently only a reaction to the permanent violations of the law by the Red Army, and it tried to protect their own soldiers from them. If one deviated from the usual military code of honour it was a 'convention of war with Eastern means' that had been forced on the Germans by the enemy and a 'return to the old convention of war' that had existed before the introduction of international law on the battlefield.[25] The Germans' own struggle, by resisting the permanent violation of the law by the enemy and punishing him accordingly, received in this way a high moral legitimation and was ennobled by the sacrifice of fallen comrades. This legitimation excluded any doubt about their own way of waging war. After the war, a former soldier self-critically recalled the consequences of this manipulation: 'I (like most of the front-line soldiers) have classified even phenomena that clearly indicated the destructive nature of this "war" into a very general – if not to say "normal" – category of warfare and military operations.'[26]

Luis Raffeiner, like millions of his comrades, had just as little knowledge of these plans for a race war and a war of conquest as of the criminal orders that had long been in place or the intended brainwashing by the Wehrmacht propaganda personally directed by Hitler when they had moved into their secret jumping-off positions along the border of the Soviet Union from the Baltic Sea to the Black Sea. 'Now we learned,' he writes, 'that Russia was our objective. At this point the name "Operation Barbarossa" was mentioned for the first time. We could not have imagined anything like this at all. In any case we simple soldiers were not given any further information. And nobody would have dared to ask' (see p. 49). Hitler's speech on the radio, in which he had invoked the dangers of Bolshevism and preached the salvation of European civilization, remained a mystery to Raffeiner.

The tank mechanic Luis Raffeiner was like the musketeer Ulrich Braeker in September 1756. Braeker had grown up in the poorest of conditions among peasants in Tockenburg, a Swiss mountain valley, and was forced to serve in the army of the great Prussian king as a young man. Before one of the decisive battles of the Seven Years' War near Lobositz/ Lovosice in Bohemia he described his situation as follows: 'I only write what I saw, what was going on around me in my immediate proximity, and especially what concerned myself. We lowly starvelings knew least of all about the most important things, and we did not care much about them either.'[27] Raffeiner, like his literary predecessor, would write down everything he saw in the years to come. With him, too, it would be about what happened in his vicinity and what concerned him personally. But he would see something other than at Lobositz, and it would not let go of him for a lifetime.

Images of horror

Raffeiner, whose *Sturmgeschützabteilung* 243 had marched into Ukraine as part of the 17th Army on 22 June 1941, experienced his initiation in the first days of the war: the concentrated fire of the artillery, the advancing packs of tanks, the armada of infantry on their flanks, the war as 'night of hell' and 'inferno'. And then the horror caused by one's own weapon: using direct fire into the embrasures of a line of bunkers to eliminate the enemy crews with grenades that only exploded inside. 'How it looked in there afterwards was horrible'(see p. 53). It took three months before he was to describe another battle and its horror, almost 1,200 kilometres further east, when the Ukrainian metropolis of Kiev was encircled and then fell on 19 September 1941. '[T]he way it looked after such turmoil due to combat was so macabre that it really sapped my nerves. In some cases you could no longer speak of corpses. Only fragments of humans were lying around; body parts were even hanging in the trees.' The usual soldiers' stories look different, they are the stories of heroes.

After breaking through the Soviet border fortifications the 17th Army had encountered fierce resistance, which slowed its rate of advance considerably. The same happened to the other two armies, the 6th Army operating on the north wing and the 11th Army in the south, advancing from Romania. The objective of swiftly destroying all Soviet troops west of the river Dnieper in large encirclement battles failed, as did the rapid capture of Kiev and the formation of bridgeheads south of the city that would enable the further advance into the industrial centres and the oil-fields in the south-east. The first stage of the campaign plan of Army Group South had thus failed.[28] On the way to the Ukrainian metropolis the Germans succeeded only once in encircling the enemy, near Uman on 8 August, taking more than 100,000 prisoners and capturing large amounts of *matériel*.[29]

Raffeiner says nothing about the gruelling advance and heavy fighting in the first six weeks of the campaign. He only mentions the names of a few towns. His unit, *Sturmgeschützabteilung* 243, had been split up for the first stage of the advance: the 1st Battery was subordinated to the 1st Mountain Division in the XXXXIX Mountain Corps heading towards Lemberg/Lvov, while Raffeiner's 2nd and the 3rd Battery belonged to the IV Army Corps and advanced together with the 24th Infantry Division on Rava-Ruska. After that the two batteries continued their advance eastwards: Tarnopol, Proskurov, Starikonstantinov, Berdichev, Zhitomir, Vinnitsa, and Uman were the main stops on this route and the names of the most important battles.[30] The assault guns – which because of their high mobility and their dreaded long-range weapons could be ordered to any flashpoint in order to shoot open corridors for their own infantry or to eliminate enemy artillery positions – were used everywhere in these battles. They supported a wide variety of units – divisions of the infantry, the mountain troops and the Waffen-SS.[31] From 19 July Raffeiner's 2nd as well as the 3rd Battery were part of the XXXXIX Mountain Corps.[32] And from 1 August, when the 1st Battery returned, the detachment was complete again; together with the 125th Infantry Division *Sturmgeschütz-abteilung* 243 was deployed in the Uman encirclement battle from 3 to 8 August 1941.[33]

But all these war stories do not interest our chronicler. He only notes what he saw happening outside the military scene: cheerful hours with the locals, a practical joke with two young women, the first Russian Orthodox service in a church in Zhitomir after many years.[34] As for his 'images of terror' (see p.62), back then he had snapped them with his Voigtländer camera during the advance and had sent them home. What has survived from this chronicle today is only a harmless few remaining 'tourist' motifs and 'family photos' with comrades. But the photographic gaze is present in his text: in the succinct detail and in the accuracy of the image. Raffeiner was close to the horror.

Already in the first days he experienced the war within the war – the persecution of the Jews. He saw it as slave labourers building roads. He noticed that they 'looked pathetic' and were 'fiercely tormented' (see p.57). Raffeiner does not say which Wehrmacht unit was guarding, commanding and beating them, but he does say that he fetched a Jew to be his personal slave labourer, to carry his heavy toolkit. In addition to the humiliation of the Jews served up by the troops as a public spectacle, such civilian 'services' – washing tanks, hauling ammunition, cleaning quarters – were common.[35] It was *not* common to say thank you for it, and with a whole loaf of bread to boot as Raffeiner did.

During the further advance he met the Jews on their way to death – they were 'rounded up and killed'[36] (see p.59). Other civilians had been hanged as so-called partisans.[37] And Raffeiner became aware of the terrible fate of the captured Red Army soldiers when they were being driven in the opposite direction from the battlefield near Uman, in rows of three, an endless procession of exhausted and starving people. When the stomach of a dead horse inflated by gases bursts and the entrails fly out, one of the prisoners rushes to the stinking innards and devours them – a victim of the hunger policy demanded by the political leadership in Berlin and carried out on the ground by the Wehrmacht. In the German prison camps Red Army soldiers, mad with hunger, would pounce on the corpses of their comrades.[38] 'May God save us from such a fate!' (see p.72): this quick prayer that Raffeiner says is not an expression of disgust or contempt for the enemy, vilified by propaganda on a daily basis as 'depraved half-Asiatic' or 'Slavic subhuman'. The chronicler's narrative is free from such racist stereotypes. It is the comment of a person who also perceives the fate of somebody else what his own possible fate could be: that is you.

Tricks of the memory

But Raffeiner also recounts the crimes committed by the enemy. After the attack on the Soviet Union and the rapid advance of the Wehrmacht into the Ukraine, the Stalinist secret police (NKVD) could no longer move the inmates of their prisons to the rear, so they murdered thousands of them on the orders of their chief, Lavrentii Beria. Among the prisoners were numerous members of the Organization of Ukrainian Nationalists (OUN), which collaborated with the Germans. After the occupation of the Ukrainian towns by the Wehrmacht the troops were regularly taken to the crime scenes in order to present Bolshevism as a 'scourge of humanity' based on the unexpected 'atrocity material' – 'Moscow Unmasked'. This was in full accord with the slogans from the propaganda campaign of the German Propaganda Minister Joseph Goebbels.[39] At the same time, SS commandos and militias of the anti-semitic OUN shot thousands of Jews in prisons in 'retaliation' as the alleged perpetrators of the murders.[40] Raffeiner claims to have heard of such a crime committed by the NKVD against political prisoners after staying in the village of Bar near Vinnitsa and, like his comrades, he initially believed that the SS was responsible for the crime. But an officer 'rectified' this and distributed photos to them 'as proof' of the atrocity committed by the Russians (see p. 59).

The event is unlikely to have taken place in either Bar or Vinnitsa, which had been captured on 16 and 20 July 1941 respectively by units of the XXXXIX Mountain Corps, the 1st and 4th Mountain Divisions.[41] The NKVD murders occurred in the first week after the Wehrmacht invaded and in towns no more than 200 kilometres from the border.[42] This does not match up to both places. Raffeiner's hint that when his unit arrived in the town there was already 'an SS unit' (see p. 59) there points in a different direction: commandos from Einsatzgruppe C[43] had started shooting the Jewish population of the town soon after taking it[44] – about one third of the 90,000 inhabitants were Jewish.[45] The recollection of an NKVD murder would therefore be a cover story for a German crime. However, such a recollection was able to fall back on actual experiences: the issue was known to all members of Army Group South at the latest from the conquest of Lvov on the night of 30 June and the NKVD victims found there. Photos taken by a propaganda company of the Waffen-SS Wiking Division during an official examination of the corpses by a military judge and an army medic on the morning of 30 June,[46] as well as the photos taken privately over the next few days, could be acquired by all soldiers. Two photos that were found in Raffeiner's collection and showing a dozen unearthed corpses could be from these pictures from Lvov/Lviv.[47] But the chronicler could also have been a witness at other places – in Zolochev/Zolochiv, in Zborov/Zboriv, in Tarnopol/Ternopil or in Berezhany.[48] For Raffeiner, different crime scenes, times, and forms of bearing witness have probably already overlapped, and with the passage of time and the changed meaning of events his memory of these has once again created a new mix for him where it is impossible to expose the original core of facts. These are the tricks with which the memory – which constantly strives to adapt to the positive self-image and to harmonize the bluntest contradictions – fools the 'self' as it does the external observer. One has to be prepared for this with every story and text about the Nazi era and the war.[49]

In the heart of darkness

After the occupation of Kiev on 19 September Raffeiner's unit had been directed north from the southern front to Army Group Centre to take part in the planned capture of Moscow. On 30 September a small group, followed on 2 October by the rest of three armies and three armoured groups, began to move eastwards. 'Operation Typhoon', the last offensive of 1941, had begun. On 7 October Vyazma and Bryansk were captured and the majority of the Soviet units were trapped in two encirclements, which were 'cleared' by 20 October: according to the Wehrmacht 648,196 Red Army soldiers went into German captivity. Already during this final operation certain parts of the German troops – overestimating the triumph that had just been achieved and misjudging the number of Soviet reserves – received the order to continue the advance on Moscow. But the enemy's resistance stiffened, the rapid supply of German troop reinforcements and fuel failed, and the onset of snow and rain made it increasingly impossible for tanks, trucks and men to advance. All German offensive operations were suspended by 1 November at the latest. They only resumed from mid-November after the German objectives had been clarified and the frosty weather had set in.[50]

Raffeiner's unit, serving as part of *Sturmgeschützabteilung* 243, assigned to the 2nd Army, did not take part in this decisive phase of the campaign due to special circumstances. Only the 1st Battery was deployed in the

Battle of Bryansk. The other two batteries reached the new operational area only after the capture of the town on 7 October.[51] But Raffeiner's 2nd Battery did not see combat in the subsequent race towards Tula either, because of the destruction of its tanks. This period of inactivity was prolonged when all operations by Army Group Centre were suspended at the end of October. The time was used to replenish the gaps in personnel and weapons of *Sturmgeschützabteilung* 243.[52] During this forced pause the surprising detour to Minsk at the beginning of November took place, as recounted by Raffeiner. One of the very rare testimonies of a Wehrmacht soldier from the early phase of the Holocaust happened all because his lieutenant wanted to have a car repaired.

On 19 July 1941 the Wehrmacht field commandant in Minsk declared a district in the middle of the city mainly inhabited by Jews to be a ghetto. It was separated from the surrounding districts with a triple barbed-wire fence, and around 60,000 Belorussian Jews were imprisoned there.[53] After the Minsk ghetto, like the one in Riga, had been designated as an extermination ghetto and the deportation of 25,000 Jews from the Reich had been decided upon, space was to be created for the newcomers with the murder of 12,000 Belorussian Jews: 6,624 Jews were shot from 7 to 9 November in three large 'actions', another 5,000 on 20 November, and a further 2,000 on 11 December 1941. The riflemen were members of Einsatzgruppe A as well as commandos made up of Belorussian and Latvian collaborators.[54]

'We encountered sheer misery in the ghetto' (see p. 78) is the first sentence of the chronicler about his visit to the Minsk ghetto. It sounds like a headline and is at the same time the summary of what happened that he later describes. As an introduction Raffeiner told us that he was accompanied by a comrade and an NCO, whose name was Seifenheld. Through these witnesses his story becomes an authenticated document, a testimony on oath. Looking for bed frames, the three of them had entered a building where they came across a large group of Jews, including a good friend of the NCO from his hometown Berlin. The owner of a butcher's shop, who had been transported to Minsk with just one suitcase on the pretext that he could 'settle' there, suddenly became afraid of what was in store because of the conditions in the ghetto and the reports of previous murders. The visibly shaken NCO told his two comrades after the conversation that he had consoled his compatriot against his better judgement and tried to play down to him the threat of death. The three of them then met this man in front of the building, where a truck loaded with Jews was parked; it was taken over by the driver of an empty truck and driven out of the ghetto. When asked, the SS men who were on watch willingly and proudly explained what was going on here: every day 3,000 Jews were being transported away for execution far away from the city. They were shot next to long trenches, layer upon layer, only the small children were beaten to death at the camp so that they did not scream during the transport, and then were later buried in the mass graves of their parents. 'We certainly knew that this was being done to the Jews,' Raffeiner admits. But this was the first time he heard of 'such a level of mass killing'. And, he adds, he was never a direct eyewitness to one of them later (see p. 79). The first sentence contains the admission of knowledge that was widely known of the planned murder of the Jews. When asked about the meaning of this dark sentence Raffeiner replied that they all knew at the time that the Jews were being exterminated and that their officers had also given them a reason: because the Jews 'subjugated the German people'. The second sentence confirms what the chronicler had earlier recounted about smaller shooting activities during the advance. His third sentence reveals his refusal to admit that he had just witnessed a 'mass killing'.

On 11 November 1941 the first train with 1,000 Jews arrived from Hamburg, followed over the next few days by transports with the same number of Jews from Düsseldorf, Frankfurt and Berlin. The train from Berlin arrived in Minsk on 18 November.[55] The NCO's acquaintance from Berlin had only arrived two days previously and, like thousands of other compatriots, was trying to find his bearings in this terrible place. Raffeiner had not just happened to witness the arrival of the first deportation trains carrying German Jews from 11 to 18 November; he was also likely to have heard about the previous murder of more than 6,000 Belorussian Jews from 7 to 9 November from his hostess, who knew about bed frames that were no longer used in the ghetto, and from the NCO, who 'already knew a lot about this ghetto' (see p. 77). And he witnessed another 5,000 of them being transported away to be shot on 20 November 1941. Nine months later the next stage of the plan, which the NCO knew about but had not told his acquaintance from Berlin, was to be implemented: for the first time on 29 July 1942 German Jews were to be shot, 3,500 of them.[56] 'I shuddered, and I was glad to be able to leave the camp again' (see p. 79). This final sentence by the chronicler contains two points: the direct experience of what happened to more than 10,000 Jews in the Minsk ghetto in November 1941, and the terrible notion of what would happen to hundreds of thousands of others after that.

On the way back from Minsk after a short rest in Smolensk the four soldiers came across an increasing number of bodies on the roadside. The riddle was solved when they encountered one of the numerous columns of prisoners who were driven from the provisional assembly points at the front to the 'transit camps' in the rear after the encirclement battles of Vyazma and Bryansk. These were death marches. The prisoners, who were already starving because of the encirclement, were forced to march 150 to 250 kilometres in the bitter cold without adequate provisions. Tens of thousands died or were shot on the spot if they could no longer walk or if they tried to flee. The numerically weak escort units had, according to their orders, a licence to proceed at will. Some commanders even issued explicit orders: 'Prisoners of war who slack off [are] to be shot.'[57] Often only a third of the prisoners who marched off reached the predetermined destination.[58] The column of prisoners that the two cars coming from Minsk encountered at the end of November 1941 was part of this large-scale crime, which can never be investigated in detail: two guards who had to accompany a few hundred prisoners of war 'mercilessly' shot anyone who tried to escape. What is interesting is what then followed: Raffeiner and his comrades, obviously shocked by what they saw and which they could only explain from the unfortunate asymmetry of guards and guarded, drove after the column and asked the two guards if they should 'send reinforcements'. The answer was a resounding no (see p. 80). Obviously, what appeared to the observers to be disproportionate was the normal, desirable arrangement for the protagonists: they wanted to reduce the number of prisoners. Until the end of December 1941, when Hitler's decision to use the prisoners of war as labour in Germany was turned into concrete orders, the Wehrmacht leadership had nothing against killing as many of them as possible. And in the *Ostministerium* (Ministry for the occupied eastern territories) the primary goal of the German occupation policy was 'to weaken Russianness so that it can no longer overrun us with the mass of its people.'[59] In addition to the genocide of the Jews, the elimination of the Slavs was also planned.

To stop being human

After he had returned to Bryansk from Minsk Raffeiner did not reach the Tula front until the end of November 1941. His unit, still without replacements for the assault guns burned in Bryansk, was subordinated there to Guderian's Panzer Group 2. Its offensive operations, however, had bogged down 200 kilometres from Moscow because of its own supply difficulties and the fresh new enemy forces. When even the capture of the town of Tula, which was to become his winter position, had failed, Guderian ordered operations to be called off on 5 December. The attacks by the other formations of Army Group Centre had also come to a stand-still in the days leading up to this. The troops were drained by the rigours of the advance and decimated by high losses. With temperatures of minus 40 degrees and without adequate provisions and winter clothing they found themselves in a state of complete exhaustion and on the verge of apathy. There was no fuel, ammunition or reinforcements and, above all – no exit scenario. Hitler allowed Panzer Group 2 and other units to begin a fighting retreat in sectors of the front threatened by the enemy, but on 16 December he refused the suggestion of most of the troop leaders to leave the equipment behind, to fall back on a continuous defensive line, and to take up permanent winter positions there: the troops were to be 'compelled to fanatical resistance in their positions, regardless of the enemy who has broken through on the flank and in the rear'.[60] After von Bock and von Brauchitsch, the physically shattered commanders-in-chief of Army Group Centre and the Army, had been dismissed, Hitler himself took command of the Army on 19 December. Other army group and army commanders, including the stubborn tank generals Guderian and Hoepner, were relieved of their commands over the next few weeks. Only when the Red Army opened a major offensive along the entire Moscow front on 26 December 1941 and forced the Army Group to surrender all previous positions in an often panicked flight westwards did Hitler allow them to retreat to the 'winter position' on 12 January 1942. From mid-February a continuous defensive line was in place and the front had stabilized.[61]

Sturmgeschützabteilung 243, subordinated to various divisions, was not deployed in the front line during the advance on Tula but instead had the task of screening the attack. When the front collapsed this allowed it to return to the Orel-Kursk area – that is, to the starting positions of November 1941 – in a relatively orderly manner instead of fleeing in panic.[62] Stationed in Maloarchangelsk, it served as the reserve of the LV Corps from 23 February 1942.[63] 'Hitler's delusion that he would have defeated the Russians by the onset of winter had senselessly cost innumerable lives' is how Luis Raffeiner characterized the first defeat of this war (see p. 81). It was not just Hitler; his generals too had initially dreamed of conquering the hub of the huge empire and deciding the outcome of the war here. Raffeiner experienced the end of this megalomania as a nightmare, as a physical state of emergency and a moral catastrophe. In order to survive he became an enemy of the civilian population, a thief and arsonist.

It had all started so differently. After Raffeiner's military 'baptism of fire' when advancing through the enemy border troops and fortifications in June 1941, a warm encounter with the village population took place during his second period of rest: a comrade played records for the women, children and old people left in the village on a Russian gramophone that had been somehow obtained. Growing up among poor farmers in the Schnalstal, the South Tyroler in the uniform of the German Wehrmacht had curiously examined the Ukrainian variant of this rural culture – the wooden houses built from readily available materials, their bare clay floors and sparse interior furnishings, the stoves on which they slept, the customs of the residents. In order to be able to communicate with the locals as he advanced he had eagerly studied the dictionary that had been distributed to the troops. That had given him 'many a happy hour' (see p. 53).

Now, only half a year later, he took the trousers and a fur hat from a dead Russian for the first time and took four more pairs of trousers from the dead or living to replace the winter clothing that had not been delivered. When the new assault guns that had finally arrived did not start because of the cold, he had houses demolished in order to use the wood to make a fire under the frozen vehicles. He knew the consequences: 'The people who lived in the already wretched buildings became homeless.' And he adds: 'War knows no mercy' (see p. 82). A little later, on Christmas Eve, he and his retreating comrades torched an entire village in order to stop the Red Army's advance. His comment: 'At home, the sacristan will be lighting up the candles for Christmas mass at this moment, and meanwhile we are lighting up the huts of innocent people with our torches! ...

The people became homeless when it was extremely cold. That was our Christmas.' And then, suppressing his spontaneous sympathy, he continues: 'But there was no time for long, sentimental reflections during the war. We had to see to it that we would get out safely ourselves' (see p. 86). Prisoners now also had to be 'killed on the spot'. Raffeiner was able to get himself released from this assignment, but he watched as someone else did it for him and saw to it that 'a Russian hut and the prisoners within it [went] up in flames' (see p. 90).

Often the peasants' huts burned down when the soldiers, frozen by the Arctic cold, stuffed the stoves with everything that would burn and over-heated them to such an extent that they caught fire. 'We were no saints' is the laconic comment of the chronicler (see p. 86). Of course, they also stole the last hen and the only cow from the villagers in order to compensate for their own lack of food or insufficient provisions. To 'organize' was their civil-sounding term for systematic looting. 'Naturally they cried when we took their livestock away from them,' notes Raffeiner. But he feels no pity: 'I had no feelings of guilt' (see p. 86).

What Raffeiner and his comrades did was to obey orders: the troops had to 'feed themselves off the land.'[64] Further, soldiers were allowed to take away fur boots and hats and padded jackets and coats from prisoners and civilians for their own use[65] and had to destroy all houses and functional buildings during the withdrawal 'without consideration for the civilian population'.[66] And the immediate shooting of prisoners, which had previously only been carried out by certain units such as the Waffen-SS or the forward detachments of the Wehrmacht, now became mandatory for all troops during the 'winter crisis'.[67] One can see in Raffeiner's account how difficult it was for him to obey these orders at the time, or to speak of the crimes of that time later on: he attributes them to the war, which supposedly knows 'no mercy' or allows no 'sentimental' impulses; it was only a matter of '[getting] out safely' themselves. The war – this was his conclusion after six months at the front – justified the means and shifted all moral standards that had been valid until then: 'In this world it was normal, it was not a crime … That was war, that was part of it, it was about survival' (see p. 86).

If one reads such sentences today after seventy years and in a civilian setting, one has to imagine the circumstances from which they emerged: for the first time in this war the soldiers of the Greater German

Wehrmacht, who had been used to victory, learned what it meant to have to flee while leaving behind heavy weapons and equipment, to be encircled and worn down by a superior opponent, to be exposed to a winter where feet turned black from the cold and frozen hands could no longer hold a rifle, with a mindless leadership that one day issued a withdrawal order promising deliverance and then the next day issued the fatal *Haltebefehl* (halt order), knowing that there was no hospital for the wounded and no more graves for the fallen. Even if it was possible to establish a front somewhere, to find accommodation, to form a defensive line, to get provisions – the howling swarms of rockets from the Stalin organs and the incessant attacks by the bombers, the constant changing between the 'at ease' position and alarm, typhus and quarantine, all made the life that had just been spared into a relentless living hell.

A scene as if by Breughel: Raffeiner, crawling into a corner of the peasant's hut, protects his head with nothing but his hands, Raffeiner, crouching in front of the brick stove, sticks his head into the sooty stove opening. 'All our nerves were shot. We numbed our fears and suffering with alcohol. During this time I drank a whole litre of schnapps every evening to be able to cope better with what I had experienced. When I think of that time, I have to admit: we were no longer human' (see p. 89). Everyone who wore a uniform was now trapped in this race war and war of conquest. Everyone, including Raffeiner, had long since become perpetrators, and now, for the first time, everyone had become victims. Both the knowledge of the moral catastrophe and the experience of the physical apocalypse had to be numbed and drowned with alcohol.

Café Auschwitz

In Raffeiner's accounts up to this point two attitudes can be distinguished, which can be assigned to different phases: in the summer of 1941, during the advance in the Ukraine, he recorded the crimes of the Wehrmacht and SS against Jews and prisoners, as well as those of the Soviet NKVD, from the distance of a curious and empathetic observer. In the autumn, when he was deployed in the central sector of the Eastern Front, he openly showed his shock in the Minsk ghetto or tried to put an end to the shootings when he met the column of prisoners. During the retreat at the turn of the year 1941/1942 we see a change in attitude for the first time: the daily experience of death and criminality in six months of war – but above all the exceptional situations during the withdrawal from Moscow – led to acclimatization and numbness. This is revealed in his helplessly apologetic sentences about the war, which according to him invalidated the usual norms of morality, and is clearly shown in his description of the public hanging of three partisans in March 1942. The event, staged 'like a ceremonial act' on the market square, was a punitive action and served to 'deter' the population present: the partisans, two men and one woman, were accused of having betrayed the positions of the Germans to the enemy bombers using light signals over a long period of time (see p. 96). As a special punishment the condemned had put the ropes around each other's necks and knock the chair away from under their feet.

It is unlikely to have been the first and – since the detachment remained in Maloarchangelsk until the beginning of the summer offensive in June 1942[68] – not the last death sentence imposed on partisans or suspected partisans there. The term 'partisan', as defined by the Wehrmacht leadership in the 'Decree on Martial Law in the Barbarossa Area' of May 1941, had already been expanded in courses prior to the attack to the effect that any verbal or physical form of 'obstruction' of the Wehrmacht, but also every 'suspicion' of perpetration resulted in death.[69] At the end of July 1941 this regulation was further reinforced: it was now sufficient to suspect a 'threat' from the 'hostile civilian population' or that someone appeared 'suspicious with respect to disposition and attitude' for them to be hanged on the village gallows or strung up on town balconies.[70] Therefore, in every place in the Soviet Union from the beginning of 'Operation Barbarossa' and in synchronization with the advance there was a court day, and the more slowly the troops advanced, the more frequently they took place. The number of 63,257 'finished-off partisans' as opposed to 638 German losses in the rear area of Army Group Centre in the first eight months of the campaign shows who were the victims of this preventive policy of deterrence – the civilian population, which had been declared 'hostile'.[71] Until the early summer of 1942, when the establishment of partisan groups behind the German lines was organized and supported by the Red Army, there was on the part of the Wehrmacht on the Eastern Front a dubious partisan war without partisans.

When asked whether he had heard of partisans before or had seen a gallows with people hanged, Raffeiner replied that he had seen it but did not record it because it did not affect him. This time it concerned him, because Maloarchangelsk, the scene of the event, had been the redemptional strong point when his battery escaped in December 1941 and had since then been serving as the base for the 500 men of his unit. The local commander, who exercised executive power, was selected from this unit as the strongest military formation, as was customary. The chronicler, who has just returned with a group of comrades from a long deployment in a forward sector of the front and therefore neither witnessed the circumstances of the crime nor those of the conviction, cautiously suggests that the three people hanged 'must' have been collaborating with the enemy. But he does not ask the crucial question of whether they were really guilty. On the contrary, the text shows an underlying satisfaction that those who were partly responsible for the terror bombing, which he himself had been at the mercy of during his first stay in Maloarchangelsk, had now been given their just punishment. For the first time he describes a crime without any scruples. More than that, he justifies it.

We learn little of the other stages of how the war numbed Luis Raffeiner – the 1942 summer offensive in the southeast of the Soviet Union and the fighting at Stalingrad. Since his miraculous rescue from the encirclement of the city on the Volga he had been lucky: he was taken to the hospital, and was then assigned first to the assault-gun replacement detachment, and then as an instructor in a training unit back in the homeland. We only meet him again in the war in September 1944 on the Eastern Front, which now ran right through Poland. Forced back by the Red Army, his unit spent the 'winter near the Dukla Pass on the Polish-Slovakian border' (see p. 120).

There, in the forest mountains of the Beskids, one of the bloodiest battles of this war had taken place in September and October 1944. Two Soviet armies tried to open the way into eastern Slovakia by capturing the passes in order to support the uprising in the western part of the country that had been initiated at the end of August by senior Slovakian officers and regular troops. A tenacious battle raged for three weeks between the army group commanded by Marshal Konev and Army Group A under Colonel General Heinrici, especially around the Dukla Pass: the pass, which Soviet units had reached on 12 September, was taken on 6 October after the Red Army had successfully broken through the Lupka Pass and had advanced into Slovakian territory. The fighting between the exhausted opposing armies did not cease until late October 1944. The losses were extremely high: the Wehrmacht suffered 60,000 casualties, including 13,000 killed and missing, while on the Soviet side there were 125,000 casualties, including 27,000 dead and seriously wounded.[72] The Slovakian uprising had also been crushed by German Wehrmacht and SS units by the end of the month: 10,000 insurgents had fallen victim to the fighting, and another 10,000 to 20,000 fell victim to the subsequent acts of revenge by the German occupiers.[73]

The assault guns – Detachments 300 and 311 – made a decisive contribution not only to the defensive battle on the passes.[74] One unit, Detachment 300, was also deployed in the battle against the Slovakian uprising.[75] Raffeiner does not mention these battles, but only briefly recounts that he spent the winter near the Dukla Pass. He had no longer been part of his old unit for a long time. After being wiped out twice in combat, this was rebuilt a third time in the autumn of 1944 to be deployed in the West in the Ardennes offensive at the end of December 1944.[76] Raffeiner had been fighting since the autumn of 1944, as he recounts, as part of the 'assault-gun detachment of the tank destroyers' (see p. 119).

His new unit is likely to have been *Panzerjägerabteilung* 152 (Tank Destroyer Detachment 152). This was deployed in October and November 1944 away from the front line in skirmishes in the Carpathian Mountains while retreating, then in the Beskids, and in February 1945 in Slovakia.[77] Raffeiner does not share any details about these battles. In any case he spent the turn of the year in a village pub near the Dukla Pass and celebrated with plenty of schnapps. His mood gives a sense of the slaughter of the recent months and the seriousness of the military situation: 'nothing mattered now anyway, you could be dead tomorrow' (see p. 120). A few weeks later his unit had been forced further west through Slovakia and the former Czech *Reichsprotektorat* (Reich Protectorate) to Upper Silesia and had taken up a position in Jabłonka, a small Polish village south of Cracow. Raffeiner and his comrades chose the *Café Auschwitz* as their quarters, whose owner, an Austrian Nazi, had fled.

For this period, too, we learn nothing about the military operations. Raffeiner was still involved in the war, which had become a retreat, but inwardly he had already left it. More important were a warm bed, schnapps, and – booty. The warriors had become marauders: in the abandoned but elegant property of the *Café Auschwitz*, he recounts, we lived and 'rummaged around in it to our hearts' content' (see p. 120). In the town they gained access to a hardware shop that had been closed up and took everything that seemed useful to them. Then they came across the luxurious bedroom and took possession of it: 'Sleeping in these beds was very comfortable, we were incredibly happy to have this luxury' (see p. 120). The author Victor Klemperer met this soldiery in the final phase of the war and has portrayed them thusly: 'the people are resigned – it is no longer a war, just a slaughter, the Russians cannot be stopped because of their overwhelming superiority, etc. etc. – but they are just resigned and tired … and by no means rebellious. They allow themselves to continue to be slaughtered without question, they offer further resistance without question.'[78]

The confession

The war between Nazi Germany and the Soviet Union was not won – although the 'criminal' orders were followed and the number of 31 million dead, prescribed by the *Generalplan Ost* (General Plan East), had almost been reached. A total of 27 million Soviet citizens lost their lives – 11.5 million Red Army soldiers, 3.5 million prisoners of war, 2.5 million Jews, and 9.5 million other civilians. This number of victims from just a single sector of the front justifies calling this war – alongside the Holocaust – the most barbaric chapter in German and Austrian history. In this respect, Luis Raffeiner's statement that after his return home he 'no longer felt like a person, least of all a civilized one' was a confession appropriate to the situation. It was also a rare confession in its honesty.[79]

As early as 1945 five high-ranking German generals had created the picture of a Wehrmacht that had remained decent in obedience and the fulfilment of its duties which was to last for fifty years. In their memorandum for the Nuremberg Trials the men stated that the troops' relationship with the Party and with Hitler had always been cool and distant, that before the war the persecution of the Jews had been rejected as unworthy, but that during the war they had had either no influence over it or no experience of it at all, and that the generals had accepted the war against the Soviet Union as a preventive war imposed on the German people, but had rejected Hitler's plan to wage a race war and war of extermination there.[80]

This legend of the 'clean Wehrmacht' became a model: just as the 19 million members of the Wehrmacht had fulfilled their duty for the people and the Fatherland with selfless devotion and kept their badge of honour unsullied, so too had millions gone about their work in the homeland enduring the suffering of war and defying the Allied bombing terror. By silencing and denying the crimes that were known to all while simultaneously reinterpreting their own history, millions of Germans in the West succeeded after 1945 in creating a new identity that corresponded to the moral norms of the present and guaranteed a positive self-image. This process of self-denazification could only succeed because it was supported by Chancellor Konrad Adenauer's policy of integrating most of the functionaries of the Third Reich into the new Federal Republic and apparently received a belated justification from the new frontiers of the Cold War.[81]

A similar immunization of collective memory against the reality of the war of annihilation took place – in different forms and with other protagonists – in the resurrected Republic of Austria. Here the enthusiastically conducted entry into Greater German history in 1938 by the overwhelming majority of the population was subsequently reinterpreted as an act of military occupation, and Austria was declared 'the first victim' of Nazi Germany. Correspondingly, it was also true for Austrian members of the Wehrmacht that they were 'involuntarily pressed into foreign uniforms' and forced to wage a war 'that no Austrian ever wanted'.[82]

This grand delusion of an entire generation was illustrated by the exhibition 'War of Extermination: Crimes of the Wehrmacht 1941 to 1944', which was shown in thirty-four towns in Germany and Austria from 1995 to 1999 and viewed by almost a million people, and this delusion was publicly questioned and permanently destroyed.[83] While many former soldiers, whose memories no one had wanted to hear after the war, spoke up as if liberated and confirmed the crimes shown in the exhibition, the majority of their comrades defended themselves indignantly against the facts: they defended the embellished image of having served in a decent organization, and denied having ever known anything about or even having been involved in the crimes. Many still defended the war that they claimed had been forced on Germany and insisted in an aggressive *volte-face* on the crimes committed by the other side – the 'atrocities' of the Russians at the front and in captivity, the 'terror bombings' of the British and Americans.[84]

But all these loud objections by the opponents of the exhibition, which were intensified by the demonstrations and bombings by the neo-Nazis, also contributed to breaking the decades-long silence. And if one listened carefully, they revealed how great the despair was that was hidden underneath. In Munich, where the polarization had reached its peak, the journalist Renate Schostack had often mingled with the crowd of opponents that formed every morning on Marienplatz opposite the exhibition site and listened to the old men talking among themselves: 'It almost always followed the same pattern. The speaker pointed to himself or showed a photo: do I look, does my brother look like a criminal? They expected the answer: no, you don't look like a criminal. Then they quickly told of atrocities they had heard of or had seen on television, immediately adding: we didn't do anything like that back then. Then the third step: we had to do it. You would have to have been a confessor to ask what they had done. But no one took these men's confession.'[85]

The reason for this was that they had not even taken the first step on the prescribed path of this ritual, that of an examination of conscience. They were evidently still prisoners of the diabolical propaganda ploy with which Hitler had succeeded in convincing the members of the Wehrmacht to believe that they were waging a 'just war'. This manipulated perception had prevented the soldiers from being able to see the everyday killing of prisoners of war, Jews, and other civilians as a crime, and from being able to feel compassion for the victims. And if, after the war, the former soldiers had had a chance to free themselves from the delusion on the basis of spectacular trials against Nazi perpetrators, through TV films and books about the fate of the victims, or triggered by public debates about guilt and responsibility, for most of them defiance won out over shame. Friedrich Nietzsche sketched this psychological drama, which is also known from more everyday situations: '"I did that," says my memory. "I could not have done that," says my pride and remains implacable. Finally – the memory relents.'[86]

As a South Tyroler, unlike his German comrades Raffeiner had not been exposed to the influences of the propaganda of the Third Reich from 1933 to 1939, but he also did not succumb to the war slogans of the Wehrmacht of 'Russian subhumans', of the Red Army soldiers fighting 'like animals', of the 'hostile civilian population filled with hatred', and of the Jews as 'mortal enemies of the German people'. Nowhere in his memoirs is there evidence of this racist thinking, not even in the total exposure of his own captivity.[87] His life in the camp was threatened by a captured

German, a former paymaster and current overseer. But a senior Russian doctor saved him not only from this tormentor, who must have seemed to him like the revenant of the sadistic farmhand on the Mittereggerhof in the Schnalstal, but also from the continued imprisonment that would prove fatal in the long term. Raffeiner also did not believe the slogans of a 'just war' and a definite 'final victory': even 'as a little man' he already knew after the catastrophe in the winter of 1941 that the war was lost (see p. 84). And he had witnessed from the first day of the war that it was barbaric.

Everywhere he encountered measures that had nothing to do with normal engagement and military craft. When he saw how the Jews were being harassed while doing forced labour, he too had a Jew help him and gave him bread. 'I could not do anything to change the situation, it was only in dealing with people on an individual level that it was possible for me show a little humanity … The expression of his gratitude went deep into my soul, it was an expression that struck me deeply' (see p. 59). Two months later, when he met the columns of prisoners from the Uman pocket and one of the prisoners ran to his tank to beg for bread, Raffeiner realized for the first time the limits that he had been set: one of his comrades threateningly pointed his pistol at the starving man. 'He did not shoot,' he notes, but throwing a loaf of bread to the begging man was no longer possible (see p. 72). In the Minsk ghetto he then found that humanity consisted only of comforting the Jews who were awaiting death by lying to them. It did not help if you refused to commit a crime and shoot captured Red Army soldiers: another comrade was immediately there to take on the job. The murder process had been briefly interrupted, but not stopped. And when he – by now already numbed to war – and his troop robbed the last bit of food from the villagers or burned down their huts when retreating from Moscow in minus 40 degrees, he who as a child had encountered hunger every day and who had experienced the trauma of the fire in Karthaus with its terrible consequences only winced inside with the verbosely justified capitulation to the 'law of war': me or you.

Luis Raffeiner's memoirs conduct a radical examination of conscience. That distinguishes him from the old soldiers on Marienplatz in Munich. But his examination of conscience lacks something decisive – the *mea culpa, mea maxima culpa*, the explicit admission of one's own guilt. There are sentences that point in this direction, but at the same time conceal the self. One was 'no longer human': this statement at the height of the catastrophe at Moscow or in the subsequent winter position or the almost identical admission during the crisis of the transition from war to civilian life after 1945 that one was 'no longer a civilized person' are such sentences. This intention to allow himself to be captured by the Americans in the event of the collapse of the front and the disbandment of his troop belongs in this context: 'If the Russians paid us back for what we had done to them, then God help us' (see p. 122). One can see in this the premonition of the usual cycle of vengeance: as you do unto me, so I unto you. But the sentence with the concluding prayer for God's grace also contains the knowledge that they have sinned against the people of Russia. Raffeiner formulates here for the first time an implicit confession of guilt and a baseless hope that he will receive no punishment.

Immediately after the war two expellees from Nazi Germany and Nazi Austria, the Heidelberg philosopher Karl Jaspers and the Jewish essayist Jean Améry, who was born Hans Meyer in Vienna and later wrote under a new name, dealt with the subject of the guilt of their compatriots in the Third Reich. Jaspers distinguished three forms – criminal guilt, which results from demonstrable unlawful conduct and is tried in court; political guilt, which follows from the political liability of every citizen for the actions of the state in which he or she lives; and moral guilt, which results from the responsibility for all one's actions, regardless of whether they are of one's own volition or on orders from others.[88] Jean Améry, who had been persecuted as a Jew and member of the Resistance and survived four concentration camps – including Auschwitz – advocated the thesis of the 'collective guilt' of the Germans. He did not mean a fact in the narrow legal sense, but wanted the term to be understood as 'a vague statistical statement': collective guilt meant 'the sum of individual guilty behaviour that has become objectively manifest' with respect to the Germans and Austrians. In order to indicate the complex nature of this collective guilt, he gave as examples of its summands 'culpability, negligence, the obligation to speak, and the obligation to remain silent'.[89] This deliberately incomplete array suggests that there were numerous other variants of guilt at the time – cowardly looking away or voyeuristic observation, approval from easy excuses or justification based on deep conviction.

If one follows this system of coordinates from Jaspers and Améry, it may well be appropriate to speak of a type of joint and several debt with regard to collectives such as the German and Austrian people in the Nazi era or the Wehrmacht in the war of annihilation. In the case of individual guilt, however, apart from the case of criminal and therefore judicial offences, only the respective individual is his own judge: only you can judge whether and how and to what extent you are guilty. Raffeiner's account of his time in the war carries out an examination of his conscience that is not followed by an admission of guilt. The reason for this lies in a problem which his entire generation capitulated before: due to the overwhelming feeling of being a prisoner of this war, which increased as the war went on, the idea of the always fundamental freedom of moral decisions and judgements became obscured and then dissipated. The generation of fighters was overwhelmed by this internal conflict and left alone. They chose as the only way out to encapsulate the phantom pain of the blocked conscience and thus make it unrecognizable for themselves and for others.[90] Raffeiner's reminiscences take a different path. They are a testimony – and there are few like them – because they point to the injuries that this generation inflicted on itself in this criminal war and that were inflicted on it at the time. And they tell of the lifelong duration of this pain. The pain that throbs in these memories is – staying with the theme of confession – the individual atonement for the crimes that to this day have never been atoned for and that will never be atoned for.

One of the most moving installations by the artist Joseph Beuys shows a bare room that is reminiscent of the pathology of a clinic, a desolate chamber of the dead, not intended for a king but for a peasant: it shows two wheeled gurneys for bodies, pushed close to each other and worn out from decades of use, including two open metal boxes with rancid fat and two used and discarded pitchforks and debarkers leaning against the walls to the right and left. The title of the installation can be seen on two slates, as used by every student in the past: 'Show your wound'.[91] Luis Raffeiner has followed this imperative with his disturbing memoirs. In addition to his very personal account of his life he has contributed to ensuring that the rupture in civilization of this war and its devastating consequences will not be forgotten. This is important, because otherwise what Karl Kraus had prophesied regarding the First World War will happen: 'Everything that was yesterday you will have forgotten, what is today you will not see, what will come tomorrow you will not fear. You will have forgotten that you lost the war, that you started it, forgotten that you fought it. That is why it will not stop.'[92]

Notes

1. This refers to the option that the German-speaking inhabitants of the South Tyrol and northern Italy would have had following a German victory in the war to either remain at home under Italian rule or to relocate to Burgundy in France, which was to have been annexed to the Greater German Empire (*Trans.*).

2. The autonomous province of South Tyrol today forms part of a territory that was ceded by Austria to Italy following the First World War. Most of its inhabitants speak German (approx. 70 per cent) and Italian (approx. 25 per cent). For ease of reference placenames are given in both languages when first encountered (*Trans.*).

3. The word *Walsche* can most likely be traced back to an old Germanic word for 'Roman' (cognate with the English word 'Welsh') (*Trans.*).

4. The *Amtliche Deutsche Ein- und Rückwanderungsstelle* was established in 1939 to manage the technical and bureaucratic issues arising from the resettlement of those who had opted to emigrate to Germany (*Trans.*).

5. The author uses the German adjective *russisch* ('Russian') to describe the local population, though technically these people were Ukrainian. It was common at the time to use the word 'Russian' to describe inhabitants of the western Soviet Union generally, irrespective of their actual nationality. Also, Russian toponyms will be used throughout the book, even when places in the former Soviet Union but outside Russia are being discussed. This conforms with contemporary German norms and thus avoids anachronisms (*Trans.*).

6. The *Reichskristallnacht* (Night of the Broken Glass), which occurred in Germany on the night of 9/10 November 1938, was a pogrom against the Jews that was carried out by the Nazis as well as by German civilians (*Trans.*).

7. The GPU (*Gosudarstvennoe politicheskoe upravlenie*, State Political Directorate) was an early incarnation of the Soviet intelligence service and secret police (*Trans.*).

8. Place and spelling could not be verified (*Ed.*).

9. The city of Stalingrad was never fully encircled by the Germans. Instead, they captured most of the city in hand-to-hand combat with a frontal assault (*Trans.*).

10. Place and spelling could not be verified (*Ed.*).

11. Letter from 9.10.1773, in Reinhold Koser/Hans Droysen (eds), *Briefwechsel Friedrichs des Großen mit Voltaire*. Part 3: *Briefwechsel König Friedrichs 1753–1778*, Leipzig, 1911, pp. 275f.

12. Thilo Vogelsang, 'Neue Dokumente zur Geschichte der Reichswehr 1930–1933', in *Vierteljahreshefte für Zeitgeschichte*, 2 (1954), pp. 397–436, here pp. 434f.

13. Adolf Hitler, *Mein Kampf*, 613–617. Aufl., Munich, 1941, pp. 739ff., 750ff., 358f., 195f.

14. Conference with General zbV Müller in Warsaw on 11.6.1941, cited in Gerd R. Ueberschär/Wolfram Wette (eds), *Der deutsche Überfall auf die Sowjetunion. 'Unternehmen Barbarossa' 1941*, Frankfurt/M. 1991, pp. 283f.

15. Richtlinien für die Behandlung politischer Kommissare [Guidelines for the Treatment of Political Commissioners], 6.6.1941, Ueberschär/Wette, *Der deutsche Überfall*, p. 259.

16. Bestimmungen über Kriegsgefangenenwesen im Fall Barbarossa [Regulations on prisoners of war in Operation Barbarossa], 16.6.1941 and Anordnungen über die Behandlung sowjetischer Kr.Gef. in allen Kriegsgefangenenlagern [Orders on the treatment of Soviet prisoners of war in POW camps], 8.9.1941, Ueberschär/Wette, *Der deutsche Überfall*, pp. 261, 297ff.

17. Erlass über die Ausübung der Kriegsgerichtsbarkeit im Gebiet 'Barbarossa' und über besondere Maßnahmen der Truppe [Decree on the exercise of martial law in the 'Barbarossa' area and on special measures by the troops], 13.3.1941; Ueberschär/Wette, *Der deutsche Überfall*, pp. 252f.

18. Richtlinien für das Verhalten der Truppe in Russland [Guidelines for the conduct of the troops in Russia], 19.5.1941, Ueberschär/Wette, *Der deutsche Überfall*, p. 258.

19. Aktennotiz über eine Besprechung der Staatssekretäre der Reichsregierung [Memorandum about a meeting of the State Secretaries of the Reich Government], 2.5.1941, Ueberschär/Wette, *Der deutsche Überfall*, p. 323.

20. Befehl des Oberbefehlshabers des Heeres über die Zusammenarbeit mit der Sicherheitspolizei und dem SD für den vorgesehenen Ostkrieg [Order of the Commander-in-Chief of the Army on cooperation with the Security Police and the SD for the planned war in the East], 28.4.1941, Ueberschär/Wette, *Der deutsche Überfall*, p. 249f.

21. Hannes Heer, 'Taten ohne Täter. Das Institut für Zeitgeschichte rettet die Wehrmacht', in *'Hitler's war.' Die Befreiung der Deutschen von ihrer Vergangenheit*, Berlin, 2005, pp. 237–91, here pp. 251ff.

22. Isabel Heinemann/Willi Oberkrome/Sabine Schleiermacher/Patrick Wagner, *Wissenschaft. Planung. Vertreibung. Der Generalplan Ost der Nationalsozialisten. Katalog zur Ausstellung der Deutschen Forschungsgemeinschaft*, Bonn, Berlin, 2006, p. 23.

23. Hitler, *Mein Kampf*, pp. 197, 199.

24. Cited by Ueberschär/Wette, *Der deutsche Überfall*, p. 259.

25. Note by Mylius (AOK 16/Qu 2), Besprechung beim Generalquartiermeister am 16.5.1941 [Conference with the Quartermaster General on 16.5.1941], Bundesarchiv-Militärarchiv Freiburg [BA-MA] RH 20-16/1012; cited in Ueberschär/Wette, *Der deutsche Überfall*, p. 283.

26. Martin Schröter, *Held oder Mörder. Bilanz eines Soldaten Adolf Hitlers*, Wuppertal, 1991, p. 76.

27. [Ulrich Braeker], *Das Leben und die Abentheuer des Armen Mannes im Tockenburg. Von ihm selbst erzählt* (Zürich, 1789), Berlin, 1910, p. 136.

28. Ernst Klink, 'Der Krieg gegen die Sowjetunion bis zur Jahreswende 1941/42, Die Operationsführung. Heer und Kriegmarine', in Militärgeschichtliches Forschungsamt (ed.), *Das Deutsche Reich und der Zweite Weltkrieg*, vol. 4 (hereafter DRZW), Stuttgart, 1983, pp. 451–651, here pp. 470–516.

29. Ibid., p. 485.

30. Regarding the general subordination of the unit to the IV Army Corps from 22.6.1941 to 14.7.1941, cf. http://www.axishistory.com/index.php?id=9184 (15.6.2010); regarding the route of detachment 243, cf. Florian Freiherr von und zu Aufsess, '*Sturmgeschütze . . . marsch!' Die Einsatzwege der Sturmgeschütz Abteilungen und Brigaden 1940–1945*, Schwabach, 2007, self-published, p. 139; regarding the route of the three batteries, including Raffeiner's 2nd Battery, cf. *Geschichte der Sturmgeschütz-Abteilung 243*, p. 3; I thank Florian von Aufsess for letting me see the eight-page report.

31. In the first four weeks of the war the IV Corps included the 24th, 71st, 97th, 125th, 295th, 296th and 297th Infantry Divisions (ID) for a shorter or longer period. The 9th Panzer Division, belonging to the XIV Motorized Corps, and the Waffen-SS Division Wiking, as well as the 4th Mountain Division belonging to the XXXXIX Mountain Corps, accompanied them or crossed their path, cf. DRZW, pp. 474f.; in the history of detachment 243, only the 24th, 97th, 125th ID and 4th Mountain Division are listed as units with which the 2nd and 3rd batteries fought together; ibid., p. 3.

32. On its subordination from 19.7.1941, cf. http://www.axishistory.com/index.php?id=9184 (15.6.2010); at that time the 125th and 99th ID and the 1st and 4th Mountain Divisions, as well as a Slovakian brigade, belonged to this corps, cf. DRZW, p. 475.

33. *Geschichte der Sturmgeschütz-Abteilung 243*, p. 3.

34. Berdichev had been captured on 7.7.1941, Zhitomir on 9.7.1941; DRZW, p. 478.

35. Hamburger Institut für Sozialforschung (ed.), *Vernichtungskrieg. Verbrechen der Wehrmacht 1941 bis 1944*. Ausstellungskatalog, Hamburg (1996), 1999, pp. 183–6.

36. These could have been the savage shootings carried out by the SS Division Wiking on the road from Lvov to Tarnopol, which the IV Corps reported several times in early July: chief of the general staff of 17th Army, by telephone to Ia [Abteilung] of IV Corps, 3.7.1941, BA-MA RH 20-17/46, and morning report of the IV Corps, 5.7.1941, BA-MA RH 20-17/277; however, the shooting of Jews by Wehrmacht units for 'sabotage' or for 'retaliation' is also conceivable, cf. Bernd Boll/Hans Safrian, 'Auf dem Weg nach Stalingrad. Die 6. Armee 1941/42', in Hannes Heer/Klaus Naumann (eds), *Vernichtungskrieg. Verbrechen der Wehrmacht 1941 bis 1944*, Hamburg, 1995, pp. 260–96, here pp. 266ff.; cf. also the eyewitness accounts of survivors from the first days of the occupation of Ukrainian villages and towns: Wassili Grossmann/Ilja Ehrenburg (eds), *Das Schwarzbuch. Der Genozid an den sowjetischen Juden*, Reinbek bei Hamburg, 1994, pp. 59–61 (Berdichev), 86 (Yaryshev), 94 (Brailov), 112 (Dnepropetrovsk).

37. Cf. Boll/Safrian, 'Auf dem Weg nach Stalingrad', pp. 266ff., 281ff.

38. Christian Streit, *Keine Kameraden. Die Wehrmacht und die sowjetischen Kriegsgefangenen 1941–1945*, Stuttgart, 1978, pp. 137–62, here pp. 152ff.

39. Elke Fröhlich (ed.), *Die Tagebücher von Joseph Goebbels. Sämtliche Fragmente*, vol. I/4: 1.1.1940–8.7.1941, Munich, 1987, entries 5.7.1941 to 8.7.1941, pp. 736ff.

40. Cf. Hannes Heer, 'Einübung in den Holocaust. Lemberg Juni/Juli 1941', in *Zeitschrift für Geschichtswissenschaft* (ZfG), Jg. 49, Heft 5, 2001, pp. 409–27; Bernd Boll, 'Zloczow, Juli 1941: Die Wehrmacht und der Beginn des Holocaust in Galizien', in ZfG, Jg. 50, Heft 10, 2002, pp. 899–917.

41. War diary of 1st Mountain Division, 16.7.1941, BA-MA RH 28-1/20; Vinnitsa was taken after three days of fighting by units of the 4th Mountain Division with the support of the 1st Mountain Division: war diary of 4th Mountain Division, 20.7.1941, BA-MA RH 28-4/7; Hubert Lanz, *Gebirgsjäger. Die 1. Gebirgsdivision 1935–1945*, Bad Nauheim, 1954, pp. 140ff.

42. Bogdan Musial, *'Konterrevolutionäre Elemente sind zu erschießen'. Die Brutalisierung des deutsch-sowjetischen Krieges im Sommer 1941*, Berlin, 2000.

43. These were Sonderkommandos 4b and possibly also 4a of Einsatzgruppe C, cf. Helmut Krausnick, *Hitlers Einsatzgruppen. Die Truppen des Weltanschauungskrieges 1938–1942*, Frankfurt/M., 1985, pp. 163ff.

44. A Jewish Council had been established at the end of July and was already shot by the SD in the first days of its existence, Oberfeldkommandantur [Winniza] Abt. VII, situation report on the orders of 22.7.1941, 1.8.1941 and situation report, 14.8.1941, OSOBI archive Moscow, 1275-3-662; this was followed by further executions, which were only stopped at the end of August, Feldkommandantur 675 [Winniza], Abt. VII, situation report, 31.8.1941, ibid.; on 22.9.1941 the rest of the 28,000 Jews were then murdered.

45. Cf. Oliver Rathkolb (ed.), *NS-Zwangsarbeit: Der Standort Linz der 'Reichswerke Hermann Göring AG', Berlin, 1938–1945*, Wien, Köln, Weimar, 2001, vol. 1, p. 142.

46. Heer, *Einübung in den Holocaust*, p. 417.

47. The two photos have the comment later added by his daughter 'At Vinnitsa (Bahr?)' and note the date of the photographsas 'end of June beginning of July', which corresponds exactly to the time when the bodies of the prisoners were found in Lvov and the shooting of Jews began.

48. In Zloczow the 295th ID witnessed the murders by the Einsatzkommandos (task force), cf. Boll, *Zloczow, Juli 1941*; in Zborov the SS Division Wiking had shot 600 Jews at the beginning of July, cf. Der Chef der Sicherheitspolizei und des SD: Ereignismeldungen UdSSR [The chief of the security police and the SD: reports of events in the USSR], no. 19, 11.7.1941, Bundesarchiv Berlin, R 58/214; in Tarnopol the same division, militias of the OUN and the Sonderkommando 4b had been active, cf. Hamburger Institut für Sozialforschung (ed.), *Verbrechen der Wehrmacht. Dimensionen des Vernichtungskrieges 1941–1944*, Ausstellungskatalog, Hamburg, 2002, pp. 100–22.

49. Hannes Heer, 'Landschaft mit Kratern. Was ehemalige Wehrmachtssoldaten erzählen', in *Tote Zonen. Die deutsche Wehrmacht an der Ostfront*, Hamburg, 1999, pp. 222–56; on the functioning and the forms of memory, cf. Aleida Assmann, *Der lange Schatten der Vergangenheit. Erinnerungskultur und Geschichtspolitik*, Munich, 2006.

50. DRZW, pp. 574–92.

51. Cf. Aufsess, *Sturmgeschütze*, p. 139.

52. *Geschichte der Sturmgeschütz-Abteilung 243*, p. 4.

53. Der Feldkommandant, Anordnung, Minsk den 19.7.1941 [The field commander, Order, Minsk, 19.7.1941], cited in *Vernichtungskrieg, Ausstellungskatalog*, p. 106; Christian Gerlach, *Kalkulierte Morde. Die deutsche Wirtschafts- und Vernichtungspolitik in Weißrußland 1941 bis 1944*, Hamburg 1999, p. 625.

54. Gerlach, *Kalkulierte Morde*, pp. 624f.

55. Alfred Gottwaldt/Diana Schulle, *Die 'Judendeportationen' aus dem Deutschen Reich 1941–1945*, Wiesbaden, 2005, pp. 84–97.

56. Gerlach, *Kalkulierte Morde*, p. 704.

57. Streit, *Keine Kameraden*, pp. 162–71, here p. 171.

58. Heer, 'Taten ohne Täter', pp. 237–91, here pp. 251ff.

59. Statements by General Alfred Jodl, the chief strategist in the High Command of the Wehrmacht, on 28.11.1941, and by the adviser on racial policy in the Ostministerium, Erhard Wetzel, on 27.4.1942, cf. Streit, *Keine Kameraden*, p. 188.

60. DRZW, pp. 592–612, here p. 612.

61. Ibid., pp. 613–28.

62. *Geschichte der Sturmgeschütz-Abteilung 243*, p. 4.

63. Cf. Aufsess, *Sturmgeschütze*, p. 139.

64. Cf. note 19.

65. DRZW, p. 615.

66. XXXXIII Armeekorps, Befehl für die Übernahme des Abschnittes Kaluga, 24.12.1941 [XXXXIII Army Corps, order to take over the Kaluga sector, 24.12.1941], BA-MA RH 26-131/34.

67. Heer, 'Taten ohne Täter', pp. 250f.

68. *Geschichte der Sturmgeschütz-Abteilung 243*, p. 4.

69. Cf. note 17.

70. OKH/Gen zbV b ObdH, An die Befehlshaber der rückwärtigen Heeresgebiete Nord, Mitte, Süd, Betr: Behandlung feindlicher Zivilpersonen und russischer Kriegsgefangener im rückwärtigen Heeresgebiet, 25.7.1941 [OKH/Gen zbV b ObdH, To the commanders of the rear army areas North, Centre, South, Re: Treatment of hostile enemy civilians and Russian prisoners of war in the rear army area, 25.7.1941], BA-MA RH 22/271.

71. Befehlshaber rückwärtiges Heeresgebiet Mitte, 1.3.1941 [Commander of rear area Army Group Centre, 1.3.1941], BA-MA RH 22/230.

72. Klaus Schönherr, 'Die Kämpfe um Galizien und die Beskiden', in Militärgeschichtliches Forschungsamt (ed.), *Das Deutsche Reich und der Zweite Weltkrieg*, vol. 8, Munich, 2007, pp. 679–730, here pp. 719–28.

73. Wolfgang Venohr, *Aufstand in der Tatra. Der Kampf um die Slowakei 1939–1945*, Königstein/Taunus, 1979; Michael Frank, *Vergessene Helden*, in Datum 06/04, Seiten der Zeit, www.datum.at

74. Aufsess, *Sturmgeschütze*, pp. 192f., 204f.

75. Ibid., p. 198.
76. Ibid., pp. 140f.
77. Ibid., pp. 167f.; Panzerjägerabteilung 152 was formed from Sturmgeschützabteilung 270, fought under this name from 9 August 1944 and was subordinated to the 1st Skijägerdivision (Ski Division).
78. Victor Klemperer, *Ich will Zeugnis ablegen bis zum letzten. Tagebücher 1933–1945*, ed. Walter Nowojski, 2 vols, Berlin, 1995, vol. 2, p. 684.
79. On the singularity of such memoirs, cf. Hannes Heer, 'Und dann kamen wir nach Russland …'. Junge Soldaten im Krieg gegen die Sowjetunion, in Ulrich Herrmann/ Rolf-Dieter Müller (eds), *Junge Soldaten im Zweiten Weltkrieg. Kriegserfahrungen als Lebenserfahrungen*, Weinheim & Munich, 2010, pp. 137–65.
80. Cf. Manfred Messerschmidt, 'Vorwärtsverteidigung. Die "Denkschrift der Generäle" für den Nuremberger Gerichtshof', in Heer/Naumann, *Vernichtungskrieg*, pp. 531–50.
81. Cf. Hannes Heer, *Vom Verschwinden der Täter. Der Vernichtungskrieg fand statt, aber keiner war dabei*, Berlin, 2004; in East Germany another variant arose with the legend of 'anti-fascism', acquitting the Germans living here and preventing a real investigation of the Wehrmacht crimes.
82. Preamble to the declaration of independence of the Republic of Austria of 27.4.1945, cited in Walter Manoschek, 'Österreichische Opfer oder großdeutsche Krieger', in Hamburger institut für Sozialforschung (ed.), *Eine Ausstellung und ihre Folgen. Zur Rezeption der Ausstellung 'Vernichtungskrieg. Verbrechen der Wehrmacht 1941 bis 1944'*, Hamburg, 1999, pp. 87–111, here p. 92; Heidemarie Uhl, 'Das "erste Opfer". Der österreichische Opfermythos und seine Transformation in der Zweiten Republik', in *Österreichische Zeitschrift für Politikwissenschaft*, 2001, Heft 1, pp. 19–34.
83. On the history of the exhibition, cf. Hamburger Institut für Sozialforschung, *Eine Ausstellung und ihre Folgen*, Hamburg, 1999; Hannes Heer, 'Die letzte Schlacht der alten Soldaten. Wie die Ausstellung über den "Vernichtungskrieg" der Wehrmacht in den 90er-Jahren das Land spaltete', in Hanns-Bruno Kammertöns/Matthias Naß (eds), *Mein Deutschland. Eine andere Geschichte der Bundesrepublik*, Reinbek bei Hamburg, 2009, pp. 104–10.
84. Hannes Heer, '"Es trägt sich weiter durch die Generationen." Krieg und Nazizeit in den Erzählungen der Besucher der Wehrmachtsausstellung 1995 in Wien', in *Vom Verschwinden der Täter*, pp. 198–248.
85. *Frankfurter Allgemeine Zeitung*, 8.4.1997.
86. Friedrich Nietzsche, 'Jenseits von Gut und Böse. Vorspiel einer Philosophie der Zukunft', in *Werke in drei Bänden*, ed. Karl Schlechte, Munich, 1954–56, vol. 2, p. 625.
87. One of the most renowned German historians, Reinhart Koselleck, expressed himself equally impartially and fairly about his captivity by the Russians: 'They treated us no worse than they did themselves. Only they were physically much more resilient than us,' cited in Eric Hobsbawm, *Gefährliche Zeiten. Ein Leben im 20. Jahrhundert*, Munich, 2006, p. 210.
88. Karl Jaspers, *Die Schuldfrage. Für Völkermord gibt es keine Verjährung*, Munich, 1979, pp. 23f.

89. Jean Améry, *Jenseits von Schuld und Sühne*, Stuttgart, 1980, p. 117.
90. Typical of this is the report by an officer of Sturmgeschützbrigade 244 on the Eastern Front, in which none of the crimes that Raffeiner recalled appears, cf. Glaube and Irrweg. *Die Erinnerungen des Werner Gösel*, ed. Florian Freiherr von and zu Aufsess/ Christian Bauermeister, Nuremberg, 2010.
91. Joseph Beuys, *Skulpturen und Objekte*, ed. Heiner Bastian, Munich, 1988, pp. 278–81.
92. Karl Kraus, *Die letzten Tage der Menschheit*, Zürich, 1945, p. 655.